FROM THE ANNALS OF ATROCITY

1868—Doddsville, Miss.: At a lynching, a large corkscrew is used to bore into the flesh of a husband and wife. Their young son is forced to watch.

1922—Indiana: Hooded terrorists put their hand-picked candidate in the Governor's mansion.

1946—Detroit, Mich.: 1,200 white-robed pickets, openly armed, mass to prevent Negroes from moving into a housing project.

1954—Springfield, Ala.: A Negro is hauled off a porch and castrated by Klansmen. Why? "We just wanted some nigger at random."

19 he House Un-Amer- e starts investigation

INSIDE
KU KLUX
KLAN

PAUL J. GILLETTE
and
EUGENE TILLINGER

PYRAMID BOOKS • NEW YORK

INSIDE KU KLUX KLAN

A PYRAMID BOOK
First printing, August 1965

PYRAMID BOOKS are published by Pyramid Publications, Inc.
444 Madison Avenue, New York, New York 10022, U.S.A.

TABLE OF CONTENTS

INSIDE
KU KLUX
KLAN

"Cowardly jackals who attack only the weak and the outnumbered, and who have earned the contempt of every genuine American."

J. EDGAR HOOVER
Washington, D.C.
1965

1

BIGOTS UNDER HOODS

"They struck by night, as they generally do, for their purpose cannot stand the light of day."
PRESIDENT LYNDON B. JOHNSON,
Washington, D. C., 1965

THE MARCH on Montgomery was over. A resolute regiment of more than 30,000 nuns, rabbis, hipsters, beatniks, college professors, chambermaids, folksingers, sharecroppers, politicians and nightclub comedians—led by two Nobel Peace Prize winners Drs. Ralph Bunche and Martin Luther King—had stormed the Cradle of the Confederacy unshakeably determined that the cradle would rock. And rock it did, for six solid hours. But now it was over. The day's work had been done. The time had come to go home.

Still-jubilant great grandsons of slaves sang freedom songs as they jostled aboard trains to Savannah, Memphis, Mobile, Nashville, Biloxi, Jackson and a hundred-odd points in between. Aging Negroes from Montgomery's rat-infested tenements limped toward their homes, their bare brown arms encircling the shoulders of Caucasian rights workers alongside whom they had marched on the capitol. Contingents of nattily dressed "Yankee" fly-ins, their shoes still caked with the red mud of the

Jefferson Davis Highway, filed into the special buses which would take them to Dannelly Airport and their charter flights north. And spine-weary National Guardsmen slung M1 rifles over their shoulders and crowded into the squat, canvas-covered deuce-and-a-half's lining Dexter Avenue—thankful to be able finally to call it a night.

Meanwhile, in the deepening purple shadows of the majestic, chalk-white capitol dome, members of the "permanent party"—that hard-core vanguard who had made the entire 50-mile, five-day trek from Selma —crowded into dusty, sun-baked private cars for a quick shuttle-ride back across Lowndes County.

The driver of one of the shuttle-cars was petite, plumpish and perky-looking Mrs. Viola Gregg Liuzzo, a mother of five who at age 39 was a part-time sociology major at Wayne State University in Detroit, Mich. Three days before the march, she had telephoned her husband with the surprising announcement that she was going to Selma with a delegation of university students.

"She asked me to understand," a despondent Anthony Liuzzo was to recall later. "I tried to discourage her, but she said: 'No, we've got to go.' She was a person who fought for everybody's rights. She was a champion of the underdog. She thought that people's rights were being violated in Alabama and she had to do something about it in her own way. That was her downfall . . ."

Shortly after dusk, Viola Liuzzo pulled out of Montgomery with a carload of demonstrators. The car radio was broadcasting news of the afternoon's march. Spirits were high.

Traffic was light, and most of the trip across Montgomery and Lowndes Counties was uneventful. Then, a few miles before the Dallas County boundary, her 1963 Oldsmobile was bathed in the glare of a pair of high-beam headlights. A car was closing in fast behind her.

At approximately the same time, not far from Montgomery, a turncoat member of the Ku Klux Klan was searching frantically for a "safe" telephone. He had just learned of the assignment of a "knockoff squad"—

a cadre of three or four Klansmen handpicked for a murder mission. He wanted to tip off the F.B.I. But he had to be careful: he had to find a phone which could not be bugged, located in a place where his conversation could not be overheard. One slipup could cost him his life . . .

As Viola Liuzzo spotted the car closing in on her, she tromped on the gas and headed for the Dallas County line. If she could reach the brightly lit, four-lane stretch of Highway 80 that leads into Selma, she would be relatively safe.

Her car lurched forward. The speedometer needle danced past 70, then 75. But the chase car still was gaining on her.

Meanwhile, the F.B.I. informer had found a telephone. He dialed the special number he had memorized and told a G-man the names of two knockoff squad members and the license number of their car. *Who were they out to kill?* the G-man asked. The turncoat Klansman didn't know . . .

On Highway 80 the chase car caught up with Viola Liuzzo, rode her bumper for a mile or two, then jolted her onto the shoulder of the road. While she struggled to keep her car under control, the other vehicle sped past her. By the time she got back on the highway, her assailant was nowhere in sight. Shaken but greatly relieved, she continued toward Selma.

At Alabama Field Headquarters of the F.B.I., a task force of Special Agents went to work on the turncoat Klansman's lead. Telephone lines hummed. Short-wave radios crackled. The job cut out for the G-men was just short of impossible: intercept two different cars —one of them unknown—somewhere in an area of 1,982 square miles. But the order came down: go to work . . .

In Selma, Viola Liuzzo discharged her passengers. Then, pausing only long enough to exchange cordialities with another shuttle-service volunteer, she headed back toward Montgomery to pick up more demonstrators. Leroy Moton, a 19-year-old Negro barber and rights-worker from Selma, went along to keep her company.

Shortly after 8 p.m., the F.B.I. learned that the car whose license number they had been given was in the area of Lowdensboro. State troopers had given the driver a traffic ticket at Tyler's Crossroads at 7:20 p.m. That pointed to one very strong possibility: an ambush on Highway 80. A *Red Alert* was flashed: Go get them!

On Highway 80, several miles west of Big Swamp Creek, headlights once again zeroed in on Viola Liuzzo's 1963 Olds. Twenty miles of desolate road lay ahead of her. She knew that there was no hope of outdistancing a pursuer. Hugging the right of the road, she slowed down and waited hopefully for the car to pass. It moved quickly into position about fifty yards behind her, then held the interval.

Mrs. Liuzzo speeded up; the chase car stayed with her. She slowed down; so did it. The game of cat and mouse continued for more than five minutes. Then, on a barren stretch of road just east of the Big Swamp Creek bridge, it came to a crashing halt.

As Viola Liuzzo rounded a gentle curve, the chase car pulled alongside her. A spotlight blinked on. There were two rifleshots. The first caromed off the roof of her car. The second smashed through the window, kicked up a blizzard of glass splinters, then came to rest in the soft, white flesh of the Detroit housewife's left temple. She fell sideways across the front seat. A fountain of blood gushed from her wound onto the dashboard.

When the F.B.I. got to the scene, it was too late. They had been only a couple of miles out of the way, only a few minutes too slow. But the deed had been done . . .

Shortly after midnight, Anthony Liuzzo answered the white princess phone on the glass-topped end table in his Detroit living room. The caller was a sober-voiced Alabama rights worker. "Your wife has been shot," he said.

"Is it serious?" rasped Liuzzo anxiously.

"It's . . . critical," came the fumbling reply. There was a pause. Then the awful truth was blurted out. "She's dead."

* * *

At 12:40 p.m. E.S.T. on March 26, 1965—a scant 16 hours and 20 minutes after Viola Liuzzo was murdered—President Lyndon B. Johnson went on national television to announce that four members of the Ku Klux Klan had been arrested in connection with the slaying. Standing on his right as he faced the cameras was a grim-faced F.B.I. Director J. Edgar Hoover, with whom Johnson had been in communication constantly since the murder. On his left was U.S. Attorney General Nicholas deB. Katzenbach, who would be responsible for bringing the malefactors to justice.

Describing the murder of Mrs. Liuzzo as "a tragedy and a stain on our American society," the president identified the Klansmen.

They were:

Gary Thomas Rowe, Jr., a divorced 34-year-old father of four. He had given police his occupation as "unemployed" and said that the last time he had worked was when he operated a bar in Birmingham.

Collie Leroy Wilkins, Jr., a 21-year-old bachelor who had been convicted in 1964 for possessing an unregistered weapon and in 1960 for petty larceny and destroying property. He had told arresting officers that he was a "self-employed automobile mechanic."

Eugene Thomas, a 42-year-old father of three and native Alabaman. He had listed his employer as the Fairfield Steel Works of the United States Steel Corporation, where he was a "laborer."

William Orville Eaton, a 41-year-old father of five and lifelong resident of Bessemer, Ala. He had explained his unemployment as the result of "a physical disability."

Having identified the men, President Johnson acknowledged "the fast and the always efficient work" of J. Edgar Hoover and the F.B.I. and "the highly intelligent and tireless efforts" of Attorney General Katzenbach and his associates in the Justice Department.

Then, looking up from his printed text, he leaned slightly forward and stared into the eye of the television camera.

"Mrs. Liuzzo went to Alabama to serve the struggles

for justice," he said softly. "She was murdered by the enemies of justice who for decades have used the rope and the gun and the tar and feathers to terrorize their neighbors.

"They struck by night, as they generally do, for their purpose cannot stand the light of day. My father fought them many long years ago in Texas, and I have fought them all my life because I believe them to threaten the peace of every community where they exist."

(Intimates of the president knew all too well the sincere conviction with which he spoke. During the early 1920s, when Klan power was at its peak in Texas, one of the Kluxers' fiercest foes—both in the state legislature and in the Democratic Party— was Samuel Ealy Johnson, Jr. And one of the greatest fears of a gangly, adolescent Lyndon Johnson was that some night robed and hooded night riders would drag his father into the woods for an excruciating bath of tar and feathers. Not insignificantly, the typed text from which Lyndon Johnson addressed a nationwide television audience some four decades later decried the Klan's use of "the rope and the gun to terrorize their neighbors." The phrase "and the tar and the feathers" was added in the president's own hand.)

"I shall continue to fight them," he said coldly, "because I know that their loyalty is not to the United States of America but instead to a hooded society of bigots."

Then, as a startled press gallery gaped in surprise, the president's jaws clenched and his eyes hardened. *The New York Times* was later to describe his mood as "sheer wrath." Robert E. Thompson, of the Hearst chain, would suggest that he acted "almost as much from personal emotion as from national leadership" and would add: "It is unlike Mr. Johnson to permit himself to be guided by emotion on matters of such national importance. For, while he is capable of intense anger in private, he traditionally has made patience and self-control his guides in public. But there may be no other public issue which penetrates as deeply into Lyndon Johnson's heart as the malignancy of the Klan."

Glaring at the cameras, the president declared:

"If Klansmen hear my voice today, let it be both an appeal and a warning to get out of the Ku Klux Klan now and return to a decent society before it is too late.

"I call on every law enforcement officer in America to insist on obedience to the law and to insist on respect for justice. No nation can long endure either in history's judgement or in its own national conscience if hoodlums or bigots can defy the law . . ."

* * *

In Tuscaloosa, Ala., not far from the spot where Viola Liuzzo was slain, K.K.K. Imperial Wizard Robert N. Shelton turned away from his television set, branded Lyndon Johnson a "damn liar" and charged that the murder was a "trumped up plot" of "Communists and sex perverts" to "frame the Ku Klux Klan."

"It is very evident that this is a pattern the Federal Government is following," he said. "It is part of a pattern of harassment. They are looking for a scapegoat. These people wanted violence on the march. After that happened last night, they went out and arrested some people and charged them, whether they were involved or not. I think this very definitely is part of the plan."

In respect to the president's statements about Klan *modus operandi*, he snarled:

"He's a damn liar. This organization has never used tar and feathers and a rope. I think he's got it reversed. He's got the shoe on the other foot.

"From all indications of what the people of Alabama have been through last week, it is he that is using the gun and the rope—his tanks and ammunition against the Southerner instead of the Klan against the nigger."

Returning to the matter of Mrs. Liuzzo's death, Shelton added viciously:

"I understand she hasn't been home most of the last several months, but has been around the country on these demonstrations . . . If this woman was at home with the children where she belonged, she would not have been in jeopardy. I notice they are using [on TV] pictures of the children crying. I wonder if the children were crying when she left them three weeks ago or if they just started crying today . . ."

Later Shelton made a slight amendment to his verbal assault on President Johnson—"I would like to exclude the 'damn' . . ."

And, that night, the Imperial Wizard—in a burst of expletive which would give Freud-oriented psychiatrists a projective field day—sent the President a telegram reading:

"Representing the true feelings of millions of Americans, I desire personally to confer with you concerning your statement about the Ku Klux Klan, selection of Supreme Court judges, rising crime rate, obscene literature flooding America, sex perverts and Communist agents within our government."

Less paranoid, perhaps, but certainly no more restrained was Grand Dragon Charles Maddox, a red-faced Kluxer who, when alleged assassins Wilkins, Thomas and Eaton were indicted following President Johnson's broadcast, declared venomously:

"We need to do a lot to stop these national politicians. A boy down in Texas did a lot already, remember?"

The reference, of course, was to the assassination by Lee Harvey Oswald of President John F. Kennedy— one of the most bitter of the Klan's many, many hates.

2

KLEAGLE, KLORAN AND KLUDD

"A fearful conspiracy against society . . . [it holds] men silent by the terror of its acts and by its powers for evil."

Report of the JOINT SELECT COMMITTEE OF THE HOUSE OF REPRESENTATIVES on the Condition of Affairs in the Late Insurrectionary States; 42nd Congress, 2nd Session, Washington, D. C.; 1872.

WHAT IS the Ku Klux Klan? How does it operate? Who are the *"real"* Americans that fill its ranks? What are they dedicated *to*? How did the organization come into being? Who were the men that nurtured and helped it grow? What were their motives and aims?

The answers to all these questions are not easily found. Indeed, since its formation, the Klan has been shrouded by a curtain of secrecy every bit as impenetrable as the iron curtain of Stalinist Russia. Members are sworn to solemn oaths of silence and threatened with fiendish vengeance if they talk. Much of the time, Klansmen have refused even to appear in public unless they were wearing hoods and masks—"to protect themselves," as one observer noted wryly, "from the preju-

19

dices of Jews, Negroes, Communists, Catholics and goddamn foreigners." Yet, though every effort has been made to suppress (and to distort) the truth, there have been a number of significant "leaks"—and, with these leaks as guideposts, it is possible to reconstruct the entire history of the Klan and all its offshoot organizations.

The Klan came into its own as a terrorist group in the late 1860s, but organizations of similar purpose and scope existed throughout the South during roughly two decades before the Civil War. As abolitionists clamored for the freedom of Negro slaves, secret groups prowled the countryside beating, castrating and sometimes even murdering persons suspected of harboring antislavery views.

The best-known terrorist group during the 1840s and '50s was the Knights of the Golden Circle. An allied organization was the Minute Men. Also prominent on the scene were The Precipitation and the Knights of the Columbian Order. All were pledged to stop at nothing in their war against the "enemies" of "southern rights" (or, as a clever propagandist was later to dub them, "*states'* rights"). All operated as "secret" societies with mysterious passwords, exotic ceremonials and far-flung networks of local sub-units.

Persons caught distributing anti-slavery pamphlets or otherwise overtly aiding the abolitionist cause were invariably visited by one or more of these groups. First offenders were usually let off with a beating or flogging and a warning; second offenders were summarily lynched. As years passed and anti-North sentiments grew stronger, the warnings for first offenders were suspended—and some people were murdered merely because they were *suspected* of opposing secession. In the years immediately prior to 1861, there were on record in Florida, Georgia, Mississippi, Alabama, Louisiana and South Carolina literally hundreds of cases where men were hanged by mobs simply because they had expressed sentiments not hostile to the United (as opposed to the Confederate) States.

After the firing on Fort Sumter, most groups were weakened as their members went into battle with the

Confederate Army. By the time Lee surrendered at Appomatox, the Knights of the Golden Circle and the Minute Men were out of business completely; the Knights of the Columbian Order and The Precipitation existed only as disgruntled and impotent bands of "old-timers."

On December 15, 1865, at Pulaski, Tennessee, a group of Confederate Army veterans and non-military students joined together to form the Ku Klux Klan. The organization's aims were more in the spirit of "mischief" than terrorism; by night-riding and similar clandestine activities, it was felt, they could harass and annoy the occupation forces of the Blue Army. The original plan was to operate under the name, Knights of the Circle; but, since it was believed that this might result in the group's being confused with the now-defunct Knights of the Golden Circle, one member suggested the name, Knights of the Kuklos. (*Kuklos* is the Greek word for "circle.") Impressed with the alliterative properties of the letter "K," members later settled upon Kuklos Klan and, finally *Ku Klux Klan*.

Subsequently, an entire line of K-initialed nomenclature was established to designate the various offices, symbols and artifacts of the Klan. The deserted mansion in which members convened was called the *Klavern*. The men assigned to guard it were designated *Klexters* and *Klaragos*. A schedule of *Klectokons*, or dues, was drawn up, and a *Klabee*, or treasurer, was appointed to collect them. *Kleagles*, or organizers, were selected to recruit new members, and *Knight-hawks* were named to initiate them. *Klodes*, or anthems, were composed, and a *Kludd*, or chaplain, was elected to lead their recitation. A *Kladd* or password boss, was put in charge of security matters, and *Klokans*, or investigators, were assigned to assist him. The only officer whose title did not begin with a "K" was the *Exalted Cyclops*, or president. His assistants were a *Klailiff*, or vice-president, and a *Kligrapp*, or secretary. The entire system was called *Klancraft*, and the means of communication, *Klanguage*.

Soon, the old-time terrorists of the Golden Circle, Minute Men, Columbian Order and Precipitation groups began to view the newly organized Klan as the answer to their dreams: Here was a ready-made secret order whose structure lent itself perfectly to the conduct of intimidation campaigns. One by one, the old-timers began to infiltrate; before long, the Klan's membership-seeking Kleagles found themselves swamped with more applications than they could handle. Sub-units, called *dens,* began springing up all over the South—and, in 1867, little more than a year after the first organizational meeting, a *national convention* was held at Nashville to establish a heirarchy of Klan leadership.

The whole of Klandom, it was decided, would be called *The Invisible Empire.* It would be presided over by a *Grand Wizard of the Empire,* assisted by a cabinet of ten *Genii.* These would include a *Grand Kleagle,* or chief-of-staff; a *Grand Klailiff,* or vice-president; a *Grand Kligrapp,* or secretary, and so on down the line.

The Empire was broken down into *Realms,* each consisting of one state. A *Grand Dragon of the Realm* was put in command, aided by a cabinet of eight *Hydras.* Each realm was subdivided into *Dominions,* presided over by a *Grand Titan of the Dominion* and six *Furies.* Each dominion was subdivided into *Provinces,* with a *Grand Giant* and four *Goblins.* Finally came the *Den,* with its *Grand Cyclops* and two *Knight-Hawks.* Some dens, fearing that the K-initialed offices sounded too ludicrous to entice serious members, were given permission to name their leaders *Grand Magi, Grand Exchequer, Grand Turk, Grand Scribe, Grand Sentinel* and *Grand Ensign* instead.

After this table of organization was drawn up, it came time to elect the Grand Wizard of the Empire. Nominated and elected by acclamation was the popular Confederate cavalryman, General Nathan Bedford Forrest. Other national officers included planters, politicians and businessmen who had been turned out of power by the Loyal Leagues of Reconstruction and the Negro Unions.

With Forrest as a figure-head, the Klan grew in leaps and bounds. By 1868, the membership totalled more than 500,000 and the Klan-perpetrated atrocities, incited by the infiltrating old-timers from the prewar groups, numbered well into the millions. Behind the anonymity of their hoods and robes, Klansmen rode the highways and country lanes, burning houses and farms, whipping and flogging Federal sympathizers and massacring Negroes. If a black man was believed to be guilty of having seduced a white woman, he was castrated, tarred and feathered, then lynched. Likewise, if a white woman was believed to have encouraged the sexual advances of a black man, she was murdered— usually only after she had been shaven bald and made to parade through the streets nude, the words "niggerlover" painted across (or carved by pen-knife into) her chest and back.

Local law enforcement agencies calmly turned their backs to what was going on. While crimes were being committed, cops conveniently happened to be elsewhere. By the time the deed had been done, evidence was "insufficient to warrant arrest." In effect, Kluxers had legal *carte blanche*—and they exercised it with impunity.

In Doddsville, Miss., an eyewitness to the lynching of Mr. and Mrs. Luther Holbert, gave this account to *The Vicksburg Evening Post*:

"When the two negroes were captured, they were tied to trees, and, while the funeral pyres were being prepared, they were forced to hold out their hands while one finger at a time was chopped off. The fingers were distributed as souvenirs. The ears of the murderers were cut off. Holbert was beaten severely, his skull was fractured and one of his eyes, knocked out with a stick, hung by a shred from the socket.

"Some of the mob used a large corkscrew to bore into the flesh of the man and the woman. It was applied to their arms, legs and bodies, then pulled out, the spirals tearing out big pieces of raw, quivering flesh every time it was withdrawn. A young son was made to witness the event."

In Knoxville, Tenn., meanwhile, Ed Johnson, a Negro convicted of rape—by an all-Caucasian jury—was lynched by an hysterical mob after word was received that the United States Supreme Court had granted him an appeal. In Jennings, La., Negro James Comeaux was lynched after he struck a merchant who had swept dirt on his shoes. And in Plaquemine, La., a mob hanged Negro William Carr for allegedly killing a "white" man's cow!

From Centreville, Ala., *The Montgomery Advertiser* reported: "Grant Richardson, a negro, was lynched tonight by a party of angry miners. Some months ago, a white woman named Mrs. Crow gave birth to a child of doubtful color. It was thought by townspeople that this child bore a resemblance to Richardson." And, in Louisville, Ky., according to *The Birmingham News*, "Henry Crosby, a negro of Parksville, was lynched after frightening a farmer's wife. He had entered the house of Mrs. J. C. Carroll and asked whether her husband was at home."

The nonchalance with which the newspapers wrote of racial atrocities is especially revealing of the temper of the times. *The Birmingham News,* for example, quite unexcitedly observed that "a negro was strung up and shot to pieces by a mob today when rumor swept through the town (of Pensacola, Fla.) that he had loaned an amulet to a suspected murderer." Apparently the editors considered the man's identity insignificant; they didn't even bother to print his name.

Nor was this patina of unconcern the exclusive property of the South. *The Chicago Defender,* not the slightest bit outraged, reported that "Mrs. Cordella Stevenson, negro, was raped by a mob of white men and lynched after she told local police that she did not know the whereabouts of her son, who is suspected of barnburning."

A particularly revolting example of mob brutality was the lynching in Rome, Tenn., of Miss Ballie Crutchfield. A mob of several hundred Kluxers stormed her home at midnight, hauled her out of bed and dragged her through the dirt-and-gravel streets leading to Round Lick Creek, on the outskirts of town. There they tied her hands with hemp behind her bloodied, gravel-pitted back; knotted a burlap sack over her head and took turns raping her; then shot her through the head and dumped her lifeless body into the creek.

Their motive? "The mob," reported *The New York Tribune,* "was looking for William Crutchfield, brother of the victim, in connection with the theft of a purse. Unable to find him, they lynched Ballie Crutchfield instead."

And, from Savannah, Ga., this unspeakably atrocious report by *The Chicago Record-Herald*:

"A mob lynched the wrong negro at Eastman, it was learned last night. The victim was not Ed Claus, suspected of raping a school teacher, but a different young negro. The real Claus was located near Darien yesterday.

"Before the lynching, the victim had protested that he was not Claus, had never met the school teacher and pleaded for time to prove his innocence.

"It is expected that the real Ed Claus will be lynched shortly."

*   *   *

General Forrest, himself, disclaimed any knowlege of these happenings—at least, insofar as the Klan was involved. Any person could don a robe and hood and commit a crime, he pointed out; until there was concrete evidence of Klan involvement, the organization must be presumed innocent. In a speech at Washington in 1868, he declared that the K.K.K. was a "protective, political, military organization" that condoned no wrongdoing and sternly disapproved of anyone taking the law into his own hands. If it could be proved that a Klansman had been involved in any crime, he promised, the Klan would immediately suspend him—and offer law enforcement agencies every assistance in bringing him to justice.

In retrospect, it appears that Forrest was sincere (if blind) in his beliefs. A year after his Washington speech, he conferred with Federal agents who proved conclusively that his Klansmen were responsible for the majority of "unsolved" atrocities in a tri-state area. Promptly, the general issued an order disbanding the Klan. Then, he made a public statement personally disassociating himself from all Klansmen and promising to assist authorities in breaking up those recalcitrant groups and sub-groups that ignored the formal disband order.

Unfortunately, Forrest's assistance proved to be useless. The Klan created by him and his cohorts had become a Frankensteinian force they could neither control nor subdue. Despite the efforts of responsible Southern leaders and Federal officials, the night rides continued and the atrocities mounted.

On February 19, 1872, the Second Session of the 42nd Congress took under consideration the *Report of the Joint Select Committee of the House of Representatives on the Condition of Affairs in the Late Insurrectionary States*. The report noted literally thousands of instances of Klan-inspired violence, destruction and murder. In Mississippi, schoolhouses had been destroyed and teachers driven away. In Georgia and South Carolina, the rate of unsolved murders was more than one per month. From Texas, General William Reynolds, commander of the Federal forces, reported: "Murders of Negroes are so common as to render it impossible to keep an accurate account of them." Records in Louisiana revealed that no fewer than 1,800 persons were killed, wounded or otherwise injured during the two-week period preceding the 1868 Presidential Election; moreover, fully 3,000 Negroes had been forceably kept away from the polls.

The Ku Klux Klan, declared the report, is a "fearful conspiracy against society . . . It has demoralized society and held men silent by the terror of its acts and its powers for evil."

Congress outlawed Klan terrorism and authorized the dispatching of Federal troops to put an end to the organization's criminal operations. Less than a year later, Federal commanders were able to report that the Ku Klux Klan had been stamped out completely.

In the last analysis, however, Klan terrorism was not the disease but merely the symptom. The *real* malady was bigotry, that bastard child sired by fear in the womb of weakness. The military forces had been able to snuff out some of the overt manifestations of that bigotry—to strip, as it were, the bastard child of his destructive weapons. But, long after the Klansmen's song had ended, the malady lingered on.

3

THE 150% AMERICANS

> *"By some scheme of Providence, the Negro was created a serf."*
>
> IMPERIAL WIZARD WILLIAM J. SIMMONS,
> Atlanta, Ga., 1919.

WITH THE DEATH of the original Ku Klux Klan, the South's torch of bigotry was passed to new hands—among the most prominent of which were those of Georgia Assemblyman (and later, U. S. Senator) Thomas E. Watson. Discarding as obsolete the Klan's methods of organized violence, he concentrated on inspiring private citizens to commit random acts of violence. His vehicles were two magazines: *Watson's Magazine,* a monthly, and the blasphemously titled *Jeffersonian,* a weekly, both eventually outlawed as obscene by the U. S. Post Office.

A study of either one of these publications leads to the inescapable conclusion that Watson was a sexual basket case. His articles and essays—devoted almost fully to the condemnation of Negroes, Jews and Catholics as uncontrollable satyrs—supply modern-day psychoanalysts with enough material for a Freudian field day.

The Negroes, Watson maintained, were literally beasts —who would gratify their beastly sexual appetites with "white" women if no one stopped them. The Jews, on the other hand, were "moral cripples" with "an utter contempt for law and a ravenous appetite for the forbidden fruit—a lustful eagerness enhanced by the racial novelty of the girls of the uncircumcized." And the Catholics were worst of all.

The focal point of his attacks on Catholicism was the confession box, which he called a "sink of perdition." It was there, he contended, that priests—"the wolves of Rome"—arranged and subsequently executed sexual liaisons with the innocent and sometimes-not-so-innocent females of their congregations.

In what may well be the Freudian slip to end all Freudian slips, he asked readers of the July, 1911, *Jeffersonian*:

"Is there not one among them [the priests] to point out the absurdity of their wearing a garment emblematic of sexual intercourse?"

Then, in another issue, he spelled out what he believed to be the priestly boudoir technique.

"At the confessional," he wrote, "the priest finds out what girls and married women he can seduce [by listening to them recite their sins]. Having discovered the trail, he wouldn't be human if he did not take advantage of the opportunity."

One can only marvel at the blatant self-revelation of the passage—but if Watson felt that it was only "human" for priests to "take advantage of the opportunity," he certainly had no sympathy for those women with whom the advantage was taken.

"No man," he declared, "can imagine a woman who could maintain her self-respect after being compelled to act as a sewer pipe for a bachelor priest's accumulation of garbage."

In the April, 1912, issue of *Watson's Magazine*, he reached a new high in psychotic sexual fancy with this nearly incredible contemplation, all of which he printed in italics:

"Heavens above! Think of a Negro priest taking the vow of chastity and then being turned loose among women . . . It is a thing to make one shudder."

Fortunately for Watson, there was no earthly way that a man could be all three—Negro, Jew *and* priest —at the same time; the contemplation of *that* combination of sexual energy and opportunity might well have been more than the impotent editor could bear.

While Watson was thus "alerting" the masses to the sexual "dangers" of having Negroes, Jews and Catholics in their midst, another magazine—aptly titled *The Menace,* and published at Aurora, Mo.—was concentrating on the political "perils" of Catholicism. Declared the publisher in the first issue:

"The Menace was launched in the belief that the Roman Catholic Political Machine, in its political intrigues and its interference with established American institutions, is the deadliest enemy to our civilization and liberties."

Subscribing to the same views as *The Menace,* but expressing them much more subtly, was an organization of wealthy politicians and retired military officers who assumed for themselves the lofty title of The Guardians of Liberty. Those things which the self-appointed "Guardians" sought to guard against were: 1) the "election or appointment to office" of any "person or persons" who "overtly or covertly" acknowledge the superior authority of "any foreign political or ecclesiastical power" (in other words, the Pope of Rome); 2) the "conducting of religious instructions" for children anywhere except "in the church or in the home" (in other words, parochial schools), and 3) the "manipulating or influencing" of the "political or social structure" by any "religious group or groups" (obviously, a catch-all clause designed to cover any territory inadvertently overlooked in points 1 and 2).

It was from readers of the Watson magazines and *The Menace* and from the rejects of "The Guardians of Liberty" (an extremely selective group, unwilling to soil its reputation with conventional racist riffraff) that one William Joseph Simmons gathered the nucleus of the "new" Ku Klux Klan. On Stone Mountain, near Atlanta, Ga., the first organizational meeting was held with 34 "splendid citizens of the State of Georgia" (Simmons' own term) in attendance. A petition was signed by all 34, and a charter was granted by the State to the Knights of the Ku Klux Klan on December 4, 1915.

Unlike their predecessors of the Reconstruction era, the new Klansmen did not focus all their hatred on Negroes. Indeed, the "blacks" were forced to occupy third place on the hate-list—topped first by Catholics and second by Jews. (Non-Catholic, non-Jewish and non-Negro foreign-born citizens were put in fourth place.)

A difference in the spirit of the two Klans, as authors Wilma Dykeman and James Stokely pointed out in *Commentary* magazine, might best be appreciated by scanning their literature.

"During the 1860s," Dykeman and Stokely write, "their (the Klansmen's) calls to meeting included such a verse as this:

> *Thrice hath the lone owl hooted,*
> *And thrice the panther cried;*
> *And swifter through the darkness,*
> *The Pale Brigade shall ride.*
> *No trumpet sounds its coming,*
> *And no drum-beat stirs the air;*
> *But noiseless in their vengeance,*
> *They wreak it everywhere.*

"The Klan of 1915 and later vintage circulated such jingles as:

> *I'd rather be a Klansman robed in pure white*
> *Than a Catholic priest black as night,*
> *Loyal to the United States, my home,*
> *Rather than the dago Pope of Rome.*"

Klan organizer Simmons, like many of the K.K.K. chieftains who would follow him, had no scruples against prefixing his name with important-sounding military or professional titles. He toyed with "doctor," "profes-

sor" and "general" before finally settling for "colonel."
Called before the 67th Congress some years later and
asked to explain his use of the title, he said:

"They call me 'Colonel' largely out of respect. Every
lawyer in Georgia is called 'Colonel,' so they thought I
was as good as a lawyer; so they called me that."
(When this didn't satisfy Congressmen, he added that
he at one time held the rank of "Colonel" in a fraternal
organization called "Woodmen of the World.")

The first few years of Simmons' reign were rough. It
wasn't too difficult to round up regiments of back-
woodsmen who felt that their fortunes and liberties
were being imperiled by the sexually dynamic Negroes,
Jews and Catholics that Thomas Watson had so often
warned about—but it was almost impossible to
persuade these fearful souls to contribute money to a
campaign that would help "keep the bastards in their
place." As far as most of the original 500 members of
the resuscitated Klan were concerned, terrorist night
rides were interesting, exciting and good clean fun; but
planning boycotts, distributing hate literature and peti-
tioning legislators were more trouble than they were
worth.

"For three years," Imperial Wizard Simmons later
told Congress, "the work was a tremendous struggle—
made more arduous by a traitor in the ranks who em-
bezzled all of our accumulated funds in the summer of
1916 and went off and attempted to organize a counterfeit order. The treasonous conduct of the man left me
penniless, with large accumulated debts against the
order . . . I was forced to mortgage my home to get
money with which to carry on the fight against this
traitor's counterfeit order and to assist in the work we
had to do."

One of the Klan's officers, Simmons went on to re-
late, said he had a solution to the organization's monetary ills; his name was J. B. Frost, and he repeatedly insisted that the Klan could be a "goldmine" if only
Simmons had the sense to recognize a "good thing."

Frost, said Simmons, "would tell me of the great
money-making possibilities, provided certain plans that

he had worked out should be authorized and enforced . . . finally stating that he could guarantee a cold one million dollars to myself and to himself if these plans were carried out.

"Sometime after that . . . he stated to me that if I would appoint six men whom he should name as imperial officers, he would see to it that $30,000 was put on a table in my room within 24 hours."

But Imperial Wizard Simmons—who, apparently, was no *financial* wizard—gave Frost a terse "no dice." The enthusiastic profiteer thereupon pulled out of the organization and Simmons was left on his own with an uninterested membership and an empty treasury.

For awhile, it seemed as though the Klan wouldn't make it. Members dropped out by the dozens and prospective recruits laughed in the hooded Kleagles' masked faces. Then, in 1920, a pair of enterprising Atlanta publicists happened on the scene and changed the whole picture.

The historical record of this particular phase of the Klan's history is exceptionally clear, thanks to the revelations of Klansman C. Anderson Wright. The talkative Wright—somewhat of a Roaring Twenties precursor of the *Cosa Nostra's* Joe Valachi—spelled out all the details of the transaction in a hearing on October 11, 1921, of the House of Representatives' Committee on Rules. According to his testimony, it happened like this:

Edward Young Clarke and Mrs. Elizabeth Tyler, co-owners of the Southern Publicity Association at Atlanta, had been "looking around for something" ever since the end of World War I (during which they conducted fund-raising drives for the Salvation Army, the Y.M.C.A., the Red Cross and other reputable organizations). They heard about Simmons' financial difficulties and decided to make him "a proposition to handle the business end."

Simmons' failure, they told him, was the result of his being a "very sincere man—and failing to realize that other men might not be as equally sincere. Instead of concentrating on potential members who were ideologically moved by the Klan's aims, they said, he should envision the "possibilities of a wonderful revival" of the old Klan's colorful ceremonials and rituals.

Under their direction, the recruiting pitch of Simmons' Kleagles was completely overhauled. Out went the speeches about "white supremacy" and "creeping Catholicism." In came speeches about Klan "fellowship" and "fraternalism."

The secret Klanguage, the K-initialled official titles, the mysterious passwords and all the other exotic paraphernalia of the Reconstruction days—which Simmons had, to that point, largely ignored—were resurrected. Elaborate and "handsome" robes were designed—gold-embroidered red ones for the officers, red-embroidered white ones for the proletariat. Marching bands were hired and parades were held. Cross-burning rituals were conducted on mountaintops. Variety shows and circuses were staged in cities and towns.

Coded greetings were devised by which Klansmen from one town could identify themselves to Klansmen elsewhere. Two Kluxers who had never met would shake hands; each would squeeze three times with his thumb on the ridge bone of the other's hand, twisting slightly backward as he did so; then, one would ask: "Ayak?" ("Are You A Klansman?") and the other would reply, "Akia!" ("A Klansman I Am!").

The "new approach" of the Atlanta publicists did the trick. Within a matter of months, a full-scale, multistate K.K.K. "renaissance" was in the works. Organizations sprang up in Florida, Mississippi, Alabama, Louisiana and South Carolina. The national treasury at Invisible Empire headquarters in Georgia was full. Night rides and lynching parties began to happen at a rate of several per week. Happy days were there again!

By the summer of 1921—a year after publicists Clarke and Tyler had stepped in—the Klan's membership rolls had swollen to 700,000. From each of the newcomers a $10 initiation fee had been extracted. Also, a fee of $6.50 for robe and hood ($7.50 if the garment were custom-tailored).

Of the $10 fee, $4 was paid to the Kleagle who did the

recruiting (Clarke's idea, to spur initiative); $1 went to the King Kleagle in whose territory the recruiting was done; 50 cents went to the district Grand Goblin, and $4.50 went to Simmons' Imperial Palace—where it was divided, $1.50 for the Klan treasury, $3 for the Southern Publicity Association. (Technically, the Publicity Association's cut was to have been used for promoting the Klan; how much of it went to Clarke and Tyler for their own personal use remains a matter of speculation.)

Further profits were realized from the sale of robes and hoods. According to Congressional witness Wright, the garments "cost $1.25," but "Clarke compelled every Klansman to buy and pay $6.50 for" them.

A financial statement, obtained by U.S. Post Office Department Inspector O. B. Williamson from the Klan's "propagation department"—of which Clarke, appointed Imperial Kleagle, was the chairman—revealed gross receipts of $860,393.50 for a 15-month period ending September 24, 1921. Further, according to the findings of a Congressional investigating committee headed by Representative James A. Gallivan of Massachusetts, total Klan receipts from 1915 to 1921 were "in excess of $8,000,000."

Nor did the newly prosperous organization confine itself to operating in the South. By 1921, Imperial Kleagle Clarke had established klaverns in some 45 states. In 41 of these states, the number of units was sufficient to warrant the appointment of a King Kleagle. All in all, there were nine, fully-operative dominions with a Grand Goblin devoting full time to the functions of each.

Throughout the South, the principal theme of Klan Klokards (or lecturers) was the possibility of a Negro uprising, which they maintained was imminent and must be guarded against at all costs. Leather-lunged orators spoke at great length of the successful insurrection of Negroes against the French in Haiti in 1803. Should such an insurrection occur in the United States, they said, the "white" man would be made a slave. Tearing a page from the book of Thomas E. Watson, they hastened to add that the newly victorious Negroes would undoubtedly rape every "white" woman in sight—after which, no "white" man would ever be able to satisfy them again (a charge the acceptance of which undeniably must be fostered by monstrous feelings of sexual inadequacy; but the Klokards' listeners swallowed it).

Throughout the North, the principal theme was the planned take-over of the country by Catholics and Jews. The way the Klokards told the story, the Jews would take over the business community (and would seduce as many gentile women as possible in the process) while the Catholics would take over the political establishment (after the priests finished fornicating with the ladies of their congregations—presumably, in the confession box). Other "dangers" cited by the Klokards were those of insurrection by the foreign-born immigrants and corruption by Communists.

Congressional witness Wright, before turning against his fellow Klansmen, had been named King Kleagle of the New York Klan and told to "give the Jews the dickens." The Klan's plan in New York, he testified, was to "practice not only moral clannishness but also practical clannishness; in other words, a Klansman would be compelled to buy from another Klansman."

Wright told Congress that Imperial Wizard Simmons' cabinet members spoke to him as follows:

"In New York City we have all the Jews; they are controlling New York; we will get under here and when we have 10,000 members here, if we do not want a man to do a certain thing, he is not very apt to do it."

After quoting this, Wright spelled out his own interpretation:

"In other words, if a member of the Klan should be brought to trial before a certain judge or jury, if that judge or jury received 10,000 'requests' from New York to do a certain thing, they would be pretty apt to do it. That was their idea of getting control of the courts."

(The plan did not work in New York, but it did work elsewhere—as will be elaborated upon in the following chapter.)

The ultimate aim of the rapidly growing Klan, it developed, was to accomplish as much as possible *without* violence. But, when goals were unattainable by nonviolent means, the Klan didn't hesitate to employ the most violent measures imaginable.

One of the most vivid accounts of Klan terrorism was given Congressional investigators by Rowland Thomas, a reporter from the *New York World*. During the three months he spent investigating the Georgia Klan, he said, he accumulated a list of 67 outrages committed by hooded night riders; these included whippings and floggings, castrations and murders.

As with the Klan of the 1860s, the "new" Klan had written its record across the front pages of the nation's newspapers—technically, with anonymity, but actually, known to anyone who could add two-plus-two:

> EASTMAN, Ga., September 5, 1919—Eli Cooper, an elderly Negro field-hand, was today hacked to death by 20 white men wielding axes.
>
> The murder took place in Cooper's home while his wife was looking on. His body was dragged to Ocmulgee African Church, which was set afire and used as a pyre to burn him. White men prevented Negroes from putting out the blaze till the church was completely leveled.
>
> Cooper had been attempting to organize local farm laborers *for the purpose of demanding better wages*.
>
> —(Reported in *The Chicago Defender*, September 6, 1919.)

*   *   *

> JOHNSON CITY, Tenn., October 28, 1920— Cooksey Dallas, Negro, was lynched by a mob here last night. Some citizens say he made improper advances to a white woman. Others say he refused to sell moonshine to white soldiers.
>
> —(Reported in *The New York Mail*, October 29, 1920)

*   *   *

> TYLERTOWN, Miss., November 23, 1920—

Cleveland Strange, white, was accidentally shot through the abdomen during the lynching of a Negro today. Strange was hitting the Negro over the head with a gun, holding it by its barrel, when it accidentally went off.

—(Reported in *The Atlanta Constitution*, November 24, 1920)

* * *

VERSAILLES, Ky., March 13, 1921—A Negro named Richard James, charged with murder, was hanged by a mob today after a jury reported it was unable to reach a verdict.

—(Reported in *The New York Times*, March 14, 1921)

* * *

COOLIDGE, Tex., August 16, 1921—The body of Alexander Winn, a Negro hanged here by a mob yesterday, was today snatched from a funeral parlor and burned by a second mob.

—(Reported in *The New York Sun*, August 16, 1921)

* * *

It was the widespread belief that the Klan was responsible for all these atrocities (and more) that prompted the Committee on Rules of the House of Representatives to conduct hearings on the matter during the summer of 1921. Klansman Wright turned out to be the star witness at the hearings—but, in terms of sheer colorfulness, the show was stolen by Imperial Wizard Simmons himself.

Wearing his elaborate ceremonial uniform and speaking in a thick, Georgian drawl, the Imperial Wizard protested vehemently that his organization was in no way connected with the violence and murder of which it was being accused. In a two-day-long session with the Congressmen, he invoked both God and his mother to vouch for his good character (neither were in attendance, of course; so the Congressmen had to make their judgement solely on the basis of the facts). In a speech that later became the model for all Klan defensive oratory, he sounded the gong of religion, rang the bell of brotherhood and did everything short of wrapping himself in the American flag as proof of his patriotism.

"I am a churchman and proud of it," he declared. "I am a member of *two* churches—the Congregational Church, and a full-fledged associate member of the Missionary Baptist Church, given me as an honor." He was also, he said, a Mason and a member of the Knights Templar, and since early boyhood had believed in spreading the word of "the fraternity of all nations, so that all people might know something of the great doctrine—the fatherhood of God and the brotherhood of man."

His performance was impressive, but most Congressmen were convinced that it was only that—a performance. Contradicting him were his own words on another occasion in Georgia, published in newspapers all over the country and never disclaimed, either by Simmons himself or by the Klan for whom he spoke.

"We [in the Klan]," he stated on that occasion, "exclude Jews because they do not believe in the Christian religion. We exclude Catholics because they owe allegiance to an institution that is foreign to the Government of the United States. To assure the supremacy of the white race [which, presumably, should be self-evident] we believe in the exclusion of the yellow race and in the disenfranchisement of the Negro. By some scheme of Providence, the Negro was created as a serf."

Later in the speech, he claimed that the Klan was "a great invisible force" that would "strike terror" when deemed neccessary. Mindful of these pronouncements, the Congressmen dismissed Simmons' brotherhood speech as just so much window-dressing. In the subsequent voting, an outstanding majority soundly condemned the activities of the Klan.

A consensus of the committee's findings was expressed by Representative Leonidas C. Dyer of Missouri: "During the past year, a constant succession of violent and criminal assaults on individuals, consisting of abductions, floggings, brandings, irreparable mutilations, application of tar and feathers to men and women, and, in several instances, murders, have been reported from various parts of the country . . . Terrorization, active or passive, of the colored people in American communities, has been one of the Klan's principal objects . . . The name, Ku Klux, alone is enough to thoroughly frighten the average ignorant Negro . . . Abundant evidence exists that such propaganda [as the Klan is accused of spreading], directed particularly against those American citizens who happen to be Catholics or Jews, has been actively circulated by the professional solicitors who have been making a living getting members of the Klan on a commission basis. (The Klan's Kleagles.) Corollary evidence that the Klan is systematically cultivating such militant bigotry is found in the contents of its semiofficial publication, *The Searchlight,* of Atlanta, the pages of which literally drip with venomous and frequently totally baseless attacks on the Catholics and Jews."

Representative Peter F. Tague of Massachusetts added to the record a statement of his own condemning the "terrible things done to innocent people in the South by the Ku Klux Klan." He pointed out that a Department of Justice survey had substantiated reports of Klan terrorism and related boasts of Klansmen, made in his presence, that the organization controlled many Southern legislators, police officials and judges. "They openly boast that not only members of Congress, but members of the judiciary, officers of the courts and officers of the police departments in the towns in which they work are members of their organization." He further stated that he would introduce on the floor of the House of Representatives a resolution calling for a full-scale investigation of the outrages, to be followed by appropriate legislative action.

"Let the country know whether the laws of the country amount to anything or not," he demanded. "[Let the country know] whether a black man can walk down the street without being molested or interfered with . . . whether a Jew can go through the street without being interfered with . . . let the country know that 30,000,000 Catholics in the country stand up and oppose their [the Klan's] actions."

As Tague prepared to take his fight to the floor of

the House, newspapers all over the country headlined the charges against the Klan. Some Congressmen felt that these disclosures would put an end to K.K.K. terrorist tactics. They soon discovered how wrong they were. . . .

4

THE MASKED MAFIA

"In some counties, the Negro is being driven out as though he were a wild beast. In others, he is being sold as a slave. In others, no Negroes remain."

GOVERNOR DORSEY,
Atlanta, Ga., 1922.

THE PERIOD from 1921 to 1925 saw the Ku Klux Klan reach its apex of power. It was a power not confined to the pasturelands and one-horse towns where the masked *mafiosi* had earlier proved themselves untouchable, but extending high into the executive, legislative and judicial branches of many state governments, the Democratic National Committee and both houses of Congress.

Representative Peter F. Tague's resolution for a full-scale Congressional investigation of the Klan died on the house floor. Meanwhile, K.K.K. recruiting offices were swamped with literally thousands upon thousands of new membership applications. During 1922, Imperial Wizard William J. Simmons told *The New York Times,* the organization accepted new members at a rate of 3,500 per day and realized $16,425,000 income from initiation fees and the sale of robes and hoods. By the end of the year, the Klan had full-strength battalions in all 48 states, the Territory of Alaska and the Panama Canal Zone. Total membership in the states was 5,000,000.

Subsequent years saw, in addition to the usual quota of whippings, floggings and murders, the following developments:

•Seizure of control by Klansmen in the legislatures of at least five states and election of Klan-backed candidates as governor in at least three.

•Enrollment in the Klan of such prominent national figures as Hugo L. Black, then Public Prosecutor of Birmingham, Ala., now Associate Justice of the U.S. Supreme Court.

•A multi-thousand-member-strong "March on Washington" by hooded Klansmen and the newly formed K.K.K. Ladies' Auxiliary.

•An increase of Klan gross income to an astronomical $25,000,000 per year and a rise of total Klan membership to 8,904,871—more than one out of eight American males between the ages of 21 and 65. (This figure is even more impressive when one considers that many American males in this age group were ineligible to join because they were Jewish, Negro, Catholic or foreign-born; quite possibly, the Klan's eight-million-plus membership was as much as one third of the *eligible* male population.)

•Klan take-over of the Democratic National Convention to nominate a candidate for President of the United States.

The unprecedented—and certainly unexpected—success of the self-proclaimed "100% Americans" was a great mystery to most serious political thinkers. Previously, the Klan's activities had been confined to rural regions of the South and small, unrepresentative pockets of ignorance in the North; now, as Gustavus Myers so aptly put it in his *History of Bigotry in the United States,* the K.K.K. "epidemic of intolerance" had swept "over literate sections of the country as well as those in which ignorance abounds."

How was it possible? Is not education an antidote to —and an innoculation against—bigotry? Yes. *Education* is. But there is a vast difference between education and mere *schooling.* And, in the words of Myers, "the ability to read," as taught in the schools, "did not of itself give the quality of *breadth of mind* and of *reason.*" With fervent (and, at times, fanatic) support of the schooled but pitifully uneducated masses, the Ku Klux Klan soon became the most feared (and most powerful) single force in American politics.

Perhaps the best example of K.K.K. power-grab techniques in action comes from Indiana, where, in 1922, the hooded terrorists elected their own, hand-picked candidate for governor and took over control of the Republican Party. The triumph, later revealed, was largely the work of one man—a Texas transplant named David C. Stephenson—who built his formidable political machine in a scant three years' time.

In Texas, Stephenson had been a man of many pursuits: stock clerk, door-to-door salesman, ranch hand, soda jerk, linotype operator and, eventually, editor of a small-town newspaper. It was in this latter capacity that he came into his own as a Klan leader; his printed attacks against political candidates who favored (or merely refused to oppose) Negroes, Jews and Catholics resulted in the overwhelming victory of an entire, Klan-backed slate. Encouraged by this success, he persuaded leaders of the national K.K.K. to send him as a Kleagle to the virgin territory of Indiana; within six months, he promised, he would recruit 10,000 Hoosier Klansmen. (To the amazement of Kleagles everywhere, he more than made the boast good—he racked up nearly 20,000 memberships in *three* months.)

Once he had a force of 50,000 Klansmen at his disposal, Stephenson began throwing around his political weight at the municipal levels. Incumbent candidates for mayor, council and school directors were told that they would either promise to do the Klan's bidding or face defeat at the hands of a Klan-backed outsider. Those in doubt that the K.K.K. could exert that much influence on an election soon learned otherwise.

Stephenson went all out to insure the success of his candidates. Klan money paid for their newspaper and radio advertisements, Klan Klokards gave speeches in their behalf and rank-and-file Klan campaigners distributed circulars from door to door. Persons who expressed support of non-Klan candidates were threatened and occasionally flogged; crosses were burned in front of their houses, and sometimes the houses themselves were burned. When the elections were over, the efficacy of Stephenson's "hard-sell" had been proved beyond a doubt—Klan candidates had scored overwhelming victories in fully 75 percent of the municipalities involved.

Subsequently, Stephenson employed the same tactics on county levels—and with the same results. By 1921, the Klan had 500,000 Indiana members and even the state judiciary was under Stephenson's control. "How," he was asked later, "did the Klan control the courts?" He replied: "By going into a campaign when a judge was to be elected and offering him 5,000 votes—enough to elect him—if he would be guided by the wishes of the Klan." In a deposition filed on this latter occasion, he also admitted organizing floggings, cross-burnings, house-burnings, the pillaging of Catholic churches and lynchings.

The following year, Klansmen seized control of the Indiana Republican Party Convention; Stephenson named all the candidates, including the governor. To the utter astonishment of K.K.K. headquarters at Atlanta, the entire slate scored a landslide victory in the general election that autumn. As Indiana Exalted Cyclops Hugh P. Emmons was later to testify, Stephenson had taken control "of everything from the mayors up."

Employing similar methods, Klansmen elected governors in Maine and Colorado. In two other states, where they had been unable to take *complete* control of party machinery, they succeeded in defeating the gubernatorial candidates most unfriendly to their cause. In Georgia, pious pornographer Thomas E. Watson—who had put aside his obsession with Negro-Jewish-Catholic sexual prowess long enough to stage a senatorial campaign—squeaked out a victory, largely as a result of his Klan backing. And, in Alabama, Public Prosecutor Hugo L. Black scored what *The Mobile Register* called a "walk-away victory" in his race for a senate seat.

A nation-wide scandal erupted in 1937, after President Franklin D. Roosevelt nominated Senator Black as an Associate Justice of the U. S. Supreme Court. Newspapers exposed his Klan connections. The stories charged that Black had been given a life membership in the Klan. Minutes of a K.K.K. Konklave at Birmingham on September 2, 1926—where Black and Bibb Graves, later elected Governor of Alabama, had given speeches—were reproduced.

Roosevelt said he had no prior knowledge of Black's Klan affiliation and pointed out that the Supreme Court nominee, as a senator, had consistently supported "liberal" New Deal legislation. Black himself admitted Klan membership in the early '20s, but said that he had resigned "before becoming a senator." He was aware of having been made a life member, he said, but attached no importance to it since severing the tie.

Some senators bitterly opposed his nomination, despite these disclaimers. Senator Copeland, of New York, in a particularly heated speech, thundered: "Will Mr. Justice Black be any different from Candidate Black, who . . . (was) backed by the Klan? Does the leopard change his spots?" But, a majority of the Senate decided in Black's favor. On August 17, 1937, his nomination was confirmed by a vote of 63 to 16.

(In all fairness, it must be pointed out that Black has been sitting as a Supreme Court justice for some 27 years. His voting record throughout that period does not suggest that he has ever been in any way influenced by K.K.K. beliefs, biases or pressures.)

* * *

While the Klan's body politic went about the business

of infiltrating the Republican and Democratic national organizations, the Klan's body militant went about its bloody business of terrorism and murder more enthusiastically than ever. In Carnegie, Pa., some 1,000 hooded Klansmen staged an anti-Catholic riot with weapons in which one man was killed, another incurred gunshot wounds and several hundred were beaten, whipped, burned or otherwise injured. In Beaver Falls, a three-year-old girl was kidnapped by a raiding party with Pittsburgh Grand Dragon Rich personally in charge. In Texas, a group of eight men was "tried" by a Klan kangaroo court and found "guilty" of being sympathetic to Negroes; as 800 robed and hooded Klansmen watched, all eight were burned alive. In Dayton, Ohio, Negroes, Jews and Catholics were kidnapped and drowned; barns, factories and homes of persons considered "detrimental to the Klan" were burned to the ground.

The situation went out of control so that many states —including some well known for militant "states' rights" postures—had to appeal to the Federal Government for help. Governor Dorsey of Georgia complained that he was powerless against Klan lynch mobs, who had executed no fewer than 135 Negroes in two years. "In some counties," he declared, "the Negro is being driven out as though he were a wild beast. In others, he is being sold as a slave. In others, no Negroes remain. In only two of the 135 cases cited is the 'usual crime' [rape] involved." Most of the others, he said, were "exemplary" lynchings, designed to "keep the 'nigger' in his place." All in all, Georgia's Solicitor-General had been able to persuade grand juries to indict only 22 out of the hundreds accused of lynch-murders arrested by police; moreover, only four of these were convicted in trials before "juries of their peers"—and all four got off with light prison terms.

In Kansas, Governor Allen declared that Jews, Catholics and Negroes had no defense—legal or otherwise—against Klansmen operating "under the protection of a mask and through the process of terrorism and violence." Whenever a K.K.K. atrocity was committed, he said, Klan leaders would flatly deny any involvement "and then give $50 to a loose-mouthed preacher who would thank God for the Klan."

In Louisiana, Governor Parker issued a direct plea for Federal troops to help put an end to the Klan's "horrifying crimes." His administration, he said, was completely unable to cope with the situation; judges and juries throughout the state were completely under the control of K.K.K. terrorists. In one parish alone, he pointed out, state prosecutors had filed criminal charges against 31 masked nightriders caught by police while committing atrocities—and yet, though the arresting officers produced conclusive evidence of their guilt, all 31 were acquitted.

Newspaper stories of the day told the tale of Klan terrorism most vividly. Space limitations prohibit the reproduction here of most of these stories—but a few are so appalling that they *must* be included:

* * *

CLARKSDALE, Miss., December 19, 1925—Lindsay Coleman, a negro on trial here for the murder of a plantation store manager, was lynched after a jury in Circuit Court had declared him not guilty.

—(Reported in *The Brooklyn Eagle*, December 20, 1925)

* * *

TEXARKANA, Ark., July 28, 1922—A negro road laborer named John West was lynched for asking a foreman for permission to drink water from the drinking cup used by whites.

—(Reported in *The Memphis Commercial Appeal*, July 29, 1922)

* * *

LEESBURG, Tex., October 11, 1921—Just before they cremated Wylie McNeely, a 19-year-old negro accused of assaulting a white girl, leaders of a lynch mob today drew lots for the choicest parts of the negro's anatomy to keep as souvenirs.

—(Reported in *The Baltimore Herald*, October 19, 1921)

* * *

MOULTRIE, Ga., July 15, 1921—From . . . (the) scene of the recent burning of a negro named John Henry Williams, the *Eagle* has obtained the following account by an eyewitness:

"There are many things about the Williams burning more disgraceful than have been published. A sick woman and her child, who had nothing to do with the matter, were beaten into insensibility and left to die because of hoodlumism of the mob. Colored churches were burned, colored farmers chased from their homes.

"Williams was brought from Moultrie on Friday night by sheriffs from fifty counties. Saturday court was called. Not a single colored person was allowed nearer than a block of the courthouse. The trial took half an hour. Then Williams, surrounded by fifty sheriffs armed with machine guns, started out of the courthouse door toward the jail.

"Immediately a cracker by the name of Ken Murphy gave the Confederate yell: 'Whoo—whoo—let's get the nigger!' Simultaneously 500 poor pecks rushed the armed sheriffs, who made no resistance whatsoever. They tore the negro's clothing off before he was placed in a waiting automobile. This was done in broad daylight. The negro was unsexed, as usual, and made to eat a portion of his anatomy which had been cut away. Another portion was sent by parcel post to Governor Dorsey, whom the people of this section hate bitterly.

"The negro was taken to a grove, where each one of more than 500 people, in Ku Klux ceremonial, had placed a pine knot around a stump, making a pyramid to the height of ten feet. The negro was chained to the stump and asked if he had anything to say. Castrated and in indescribable torture, the negro asked for a cigarette, lit it and blew the smoke in the face of his tormenters.

"The pyre was lit and a hundred men and women, old and young, grandmothers among them, joined hands and danced around the negro while he burned, and began to sing 'Nearer My God to Thee.' "

—(Reported in *The Washington Eagle*, July 16, 1921)

* * *

OSCEOLA, Ark., June 2, 1926—Albert Blades, 22-year-old negro, was hanged and burned for allegedly attacking a small white girl. Doctors examined the child today and said that she had not been attacked. It appears that the child had merely been startled by Blades while she was playing.

—(Reported in *The St. Louis Argus*, June 8, 1926)

* * *

MILLEDGEVILLE, Ga., February 16, 1923—Fingers and ears of two negroes who were lynched near this city last week are now on display in a large bottle filled with alcohol on the counter of the town drug store. An inscription near the bottle says:

"What's left of the niggers that shot a white man."

Lindsey B. Gilmore, a white grocer, was shot when he took after two negroes, unidentified, who were caught stealing cheese and cash from Gilmore's store. A number of witnesses have stated that in the chase Gilmore was shot by a local officer whose aim was faulty.

—(Reported in *The Chicago Defender*, February 17, 1923)

* * *

COLUMBIA, Mo., April 19, 1923—A mob of 500—consisting mainly of university students—lynched James T. Scott, a negro janitor at the University of Missouri, who was accused of attempting to assault the daughter of the head of the German department . . . His neck snapped audibly.

—(Reported in *The New York World*, April 20, 1923)

* * *

HELENA, Ark., November 18, 1921—August Turner, negro, was summoned to remove the charred remains of his son William, 19, who was cremated at a bonfire in front of city hall last night.

—Reported in *The St. Louis Argus,* November 25, 1921)

*   *   *

COLUMBIA, Tenn., November 12, 1927—The balcony of a courthouse became a gallows for Henry Choate, 18-year-old negro accused of attacking a white girl. A mob hanged him from the balustrade, which was still festooned with flags and bunting from yesterday's Armistice Day celebration.

—(Reported in *The New York World,* November 12, 1927)

*   *   *

As K.K.K. terrorism continued, K.K.K. recruiting drives chalked up more and more members. Kleagles staged lavish parades, extravagant variety shows and extraordinarily elaborate ceremonials. On occasion, the castration and lynching of an innocent Negro was the highlight of a Klavern's initiation festivities. By the end of 1924, Invisible Empire headquarters at Atlanta was claiming 8,000,000 memberships—and Imperial Kleagle Clarke boasted of more than $100,000,000 gross earnings.

One of the casualties of the Klan's new-found affluence was Imperial Wizard Simmons. In 1923, he was summarily given the gate—and hastily proceeded to blame his misfortune on greedy members of his cabinet. "The men who ruthlessly took charge," he told *The New York Times,* "were moved by selfish aggrandizement, a desire for graft. They created a condition I could not endorse."

(Affidavits in a Federal Court suggested that Simmons sold his interest in the Klan—for $146,000. He, himself, admitted later that he was paid $90,000, but insisted that he spent it all forming a new organization, "Knights of the Flaming Sword." His "Knights" floundered around for six months as a powerless pseudo-Klan, then collapsed. In 1930, he tried again—with an organization called The White Band, dedicated to the preservation of "white supremacy in America." His luck had not improved, and, by January of 1931, both Simmons *and* his White Band had faded out of the national spotlight, never to return again.)

The new Imperial Wizard of the Invisible Empire was one Hiram Wesley Evans, a cabinet member under the Simmons regime. Like the bogus "colonel" who preceded him, he had no qualms about assuming a lofty professional title. He became "Doctor Evans," and even fooled a good many of his own fellow Klansmen. "I thought he was a doctor of divinity when I joined the organization, and that is one of the things that had a lot of influence with me," Indiana Grand Dragon of the Realm Hugh P. Emmons was to testify later. "(I found out) he was a dentist; he had a little one-chair shop in Georgia." Actually, Evans' one-chair shop was in Dallas, Tex.—and, from the moment he took over as Imperial Wizard, he began spending Klan money as if he were trying to make the oil millionaires "back home" look like pikers. In a suit filed by five Pennsylvania Klansmen, the Evans regime was accused of having misused $15,000,000 collected in the Keystone State alone—none of which ever found its way to the Klan treasury. Part of the amount, the Pennsylvanians charged, was used for building a lavish "imperial palace" which Evans made his Atlanta home; a lesser sum was used to purchase "a diamond tiara, valued at $30,000 to $100,000, for the Imperial Commander, or chief officer of women, of the Klan (Ladies' Auxiliary)."

It was under Evans' direction that the Klansmen and their Auxiliary marched on the Capitol Building in Washington in a "show of strength." And it was under his personal supervision—with able assistance from Imperial Kleagle Clarke—that the Klan took over the 1924 Democratic National Convention.

The aims of the Convention insurrectionists were two: 1) to block the nomination as presidential candidate of New York Governor Alfred E. Smith, a Roman Catholic, and 2) to defeat an attempt (sure to be made) by

Northern liberals to insert a plank in the party platform condemning the Klan by name.

For months prior to the convention, Klansmen worked quietly and diligently to load the various state delegations with men who would be sure to do their bidding. In some cases, they succeeded in getting fellow Klansmen named as delegates; when this wasn't possible, they used conventional persuasive tactics—cross-burnings, whippings, floggings and threats of more violent punishments—to enlist non-Klansmen delegates to their cause. By the time the chairman's gavel was rapped to signify the convention's beginning, Imperial Wizard Evans' henchmen were able to advise him that some 450 delegates were "in the bag" and another 100— enough for a slim majority—were "on the fence, but leaning toward us."

Blocking Smith's presidential bid didn't prove to be very difficult. Senator Watson's followers persuaded a number of delegates that, even if they *weren't* anti-Catholic, they should realize that a Catholic could never win the election. Anonymous Klansmen convinced other delegates that, if they voted for Smith, their homes and families would fall victim to the well-known K.K.K. vengeance techniques. These groups, added to those already opposed to Smith because of their own anti-Catholic prejudices—or, in some cases, because they felt he was not the man best qualified to represent their party—were enough to do the job. Despite an impassioned plea for Smith by wheelchair-bound Franklin D. Roosevelt, the convention chose one J. W. Davis as its candidate. (He was soundly defeated in November by the Republican incumbent, Calvin Coolidge.)

The platform proved to be a more difficult enterprise. The fiery W. R. Pattangall, leader of the Maine delegation, was determined that he would force the convention to adopt a plank condemning the Klan by name. The Resolutions Committee, eager to avert any interparty warfare, had attempted to mollify him with a plank that would condemn "any effort to arouse racial or religious dissensions." But Pattangall refused to compromise, and, when the Resolutions Committee adopted by two-thirds majority the conciliatory, no-name plank, the irate Maine leader took his battle to the convention floor.

In a heated, arm-waving and fist-pounding speech, he lashed out at the Klan as the greatest threat—internal or external—to America's freedom. He demanded, with the support of 13 other members of the Resolutions Committee, the acceptance of a minority report. The Democratic Party, he insisted, should insert in its platform an explicit pledge "to oppose any effort on the part of the *Ku Klux Klan or any organization* to interfere with the religious liberty or political freedom (of the people)."

In the tense floor-fight that followed, the Pattangall plank was defeated by the slim margin of 546.15 to 542.85. The Democratic National Convention condemned only "any effort" to arouse "dissension."

It had been close, but it had worked. The Klan had blocked both the Smith bid and the Pattangall plank. It had, in every sense of the term, actually *taken over* the Democratic National Convention. At the Imperial Palace in Atlanta, Wizard Evans called for a celebration. Bootleg liquor flowed freely. Exuberant Klansmen congratulated each other on their *coup*. It wouldn't be long, some felt, before the entire United States would be run by the Ku Klux Klan.

Little did they realize, as of that moment, that they had passed their zenith. From then on, the only way to go was down!

5

DECLINE AND FALL
OF AN EMPIRE

"The one thing the Klan has accomplished thus far has been the enrichment in money and power of certain persons who, before it was originated, had neither."

W. R. PATTANGALL,
Bangor, Me., 1928.

ON A BRISK OCTOBER MORNING, Imperial Wizard Hiram W. Evans mounted a podium in his home town of Dallas, Tex., and delivered a typically venomous K.K.K. tirade against Catholics, Negroes and Jews. The Catholics, he declared, were un-American because, to them, "the presidency at Washington is subordinate to the priesthood at Rome"; the Negroes, meanwhile, had brought to America "the low mentality of savage (African) ancestors"; and the Jews could not "attain the Anglo-Saxon level" of patriotism because they contained within themselves an "absolutely unblendable element." All told, he concluded, the three groups could not truly be considered Americans because they defied "every fundamental requirement of assimilation" into Anglo-Saxon society; only the White Anglo-Saxon Protestants of the Klan could truly claim "100% Americanism."

Having made these pronouncements, the Imperial Wizard led a regiment of cross-carrying Kluxers through the streets of the city; as they marched, they sang "Onward Christian Soldiers" to the beat of a 60-piece band.

The ceremony and speech were hardly unusual; similar nonsense had been a part of klankraft for 60 years. But, in a sense, this particular ceremony and speech in Dallas were especially significant—because here, for the first time, the top-ranking officer of the Klan had hurled his vile imprecations before the microphones of the country's major radio networks and in the presence of a complete complement of newsmen.

No longer could the K.K.K. claim brotherhood and fraternalism; no longer could it dismiss anti-Negro, anti-Catholic, and anti-Jewish preachments as the work of radicals outside its ranks; the speech was on record and the Klan's official doctrine of hate was perfectly clear: it had come straight from the horse's mouth (or as one newsman put it, "from the opposite end of that animal's anatomy").

The National Catholic Welfare Conference and the Executive Committee of Orthodox Rabbis of America fired off quick replies to the Imperial Wizard. Evans' speech, declared the Rev. William Burke of the NCWC, proved finally the intolerance the Klan had so long denied. If Evans wanted to debate Americanism, added Rabbi Simon Glazer of ECORA, the Jews he had declared as his enemies would be happy to engage him at his earliest convenience.

Evans ignored the clerics' replies—but the clerics didn't ignore him. A few weeks later, they met in Washington with a group of distinguished educators, businessmen and political leaders and formed The National Vigilance Association—whose sole, expressed purpose was to fight the Ku Klux Klan. The first goal of the association, it was announced, would be to solicit the formal condemnation of the Klan by fraternal orders, civic and labor organizations and prominent private citizens; the second goal would be to bring about legislative action to prevent further acts of K.K.K. terrorism.

President Calvin Coolidge promptly responded to the NVA plea with a resolution soundly condemning the Klan and promising to lend all the powers of his office to bringing accused terrorists to justice. The American Federation of Labor and the United Mineworkers Union warned that any member found guilty of belonging to the Klan would immediately lose union membership and all accompanying or accrued benefits. The American Legion, sharply condemning both the Klan and the feeble law enforcements which enabled it to operate, offered $3,000 rewards for any information leading to the arrest and conviction of Klan criminals.

The New York State Legislature, prodded by Governor Al Smith and by Franklin D. Roosevelt, passed a law requiring all organizations except those chartered as labor unions or benevolent orders to make public their regulations, oaths and membership rosters; it further decreed that to knowingly affiliate with any organization failing to comply with this statute would be a misdemeanor. (The K.K.K., contending that this was discriminatory, brought suit against the State seeking to have the law declared unconstitutional; the law was upheld both by New York courts and the U. S. Supreme Court.) The states of Iowa, Texas, Minnesota and Michigan passed similar laws, plus statutes forbidding the wearing of hoods or masks on highways or public thoroughfares. Other states followed suit.

In Oregon, where the Klan-controlled legislature had passed a law compelling all parents to send their children to public schools (thereby, crippling the parochial schools of the Catholic and Jewish faiths), a Federal court declared the law unconstitutional. The Supreme Court of the United States upheld the decision.

In Alabama, Attorney General James McCall resigned his own Klan membership and immediately cracked down on his former confreres. In Covington, La., Judge Prentiss B. Carter called for a special Grand Jury to deal with mob violence. And, in Herrin, Ill., a group of private citizens—fed up with lax law enforcement and an indifferent judiciary—greeted night-riding Klansmen with a dose of their own medicine: A platoon of masked Kluxers, formed to harass a local anti-Klan businessman, was cut down in the street by rifle fire from a squad of the Herrin Self-Protective Association; three Kluxers died, another dozen were injured.

Indiana, meanwhile, brought first-degree murder charges against wheeler-dealer David Stephenson. Shortly after his first wife, whom he had divorced and remarried, appeared on the scene in Indianapolis, a local girl named Madge Oberholtzer—believed to be his mistress—was found shot to death. Stephenson was arrested largely as a result of testimony by fellow Klansmen, whose animosity, it is said, he incurred by pocketing much of the K.K.K. revenues. Brought to trial in a court he had so very recently controlled, the one-time scourge of the Hoosier hills was sentenced to life imprisonment.

Stephenson maintained steadfastly that he was doublecrossed, and a year later, in 1927, he turned the tables on the Klan—by admitting to all anti-Klan accusations and exposing by name those who had been involved with him in the whippings, floggings, house burnings and murders that accompanied the power grab of the early '20s. But, if this ploy was intended to result in his freedom, it fell considerably wide of the mark—because he spent the next 25 years behind bars.

*   *   *

With the public confessions of David C. Stephenson, the Klan was on the run—and it was running scared. During 1926, like the well-known rats deserting a sinking ship, no fewer than 6,000,000 Kluxers left the organization. By the end of the following year, an additional 750,000 fled. Now, Imperial Wizard Evans—who two years before had boasted that his membership would soon reach the 10,000,000 mark—found himself with a scant 321,000 die-hards on the rolls.

The final blow—and proverbial straw that broke the camel's back—came in Pennsylvania during April of 1928. A year previously, the Invisible Empire had brought suit against five ex-members—one time higher-ups in the Klan organization, more recently deserters—seeking to enjoin them from using the word, "Klan," in a new organization they had formed; further, the suit asked $100,000 in damages, representing funds the quintet had collected while using the name "Klan." The Pennsylvanians had replied with the counter-suit cited in the previous chapter, charging Evans with misusing $15,000,000 in Klan funds and implicating him in riots, floggings, kidnappings and murders. The case came to trial on April 9, 1928, before Judge W. H. S. Thomson.

Heading the Pennsylvanians' legal battery was attorney Van A. Barrickman, who immediately lashed out at Imperial Wizard Evans as a "monster" who had transformed the "once-innocent" Klan into an organization "supreme in its rottenness." Evans, he declared, "came from Dallas, Texas, (as) a poor man who could not even pay his office rent. Now he wears sparkling diamonds, lives in splendor at the seat of the country's Government in Washington, and, when seeking recreation, whiles his time away aboard his palatial yacht—which is always at his beck and call on the Potomac."

Evidence was then introduced implicating the Klan, Imperial Wizard Evans and other officers in crimes committed throughout the tri-state area of Pennsylvania, New Jersey and Ohio. The Pennsylvania Klan's Captain J. R. Ramsey—one of the few Kluxers whose use of a military title was legitimate (he earned it in the Spanish-American War)—admitted he had led parties of night-riders on raids on Dayton, Ohio; the raids, he said, were dispatched by Evans, Grand Dragon Rich of Pittsburgh and other Klan officers and included "burning barns, tar-and-feather parties and other ruthlessness." Other Klansmen spelled out the details of a "castration party" in Beaver Falls, Pa., on July 6, 1923, where two Negroes were brutally flogged before being desexed and burned to death. Still other Klansmen testified that Grand Dragon Rich personally took part in the kidnapping of a three-year-old Pittsburgh girl, and that both Rich and Evans had arranged the kidnapping of Jews throughout Pennsylvania and Ohio.

The strongest evidence against Evans, however, involved the riot at Carnegie, Pa., on August 25, 1923. Evans, witnesses swore, had martialled some 1,000 robed Klansmen to parade in that steel-manufacturing center in an attempt to entice nonmembers to join the Klan and also to harass the city's large population of Roman Catholics. Municipal officials, testimony continued, had learned of the planned parade and issued a formal order prohibiting it; but Evans had massed his troops at the boundary of the city, prepared to give his marching orders.

The Police Chief of Carnegie, it was further testified, hurried to the city line and personally commanded the Klansmen to disperse. Evans hesitated momentarily, then defied the chief and issued the order to march; Klansmen swept down upon the town, setting fire to buildings, shooting at police and private citizens, breaking store windows and overturning automobiles. At least two men were injured by bullets—one mortally— and countless hundreds were beaten, stabbed or otherwise injured.

Moreover, witnesses testified, Evans and Rich later "rejoiced" about the Carnegie riots—and they suggested staging additional ones in other parts of the state as a method of increasing memberships.

Testifying in his own behalf, Evans denied most of the charges—but admitted that he had the power to stop the Carnegie riots, and said that he chose not to stop them because "it wasn't my responsibility." The chief attorney of the Klan's legal team offered a closing argument which, ignoring the evidence of atrocities against Evans and the K.K.K., insisted that the judge rule on the questions of the suit and counter-suit.

The questions before the court were: 1) Should the "banished" Pennsylvania Klansmen be ordered to cease using the name "Klan" and be made to pay $100,000 damages, or 2) Should Evans and the Klan be found guilty of having misused $15,000,000 of the Pennsylvania Klan's funds.

Judge Thomson flatly dismissed both suits. Evans and his Invisible Empire, he declared, had by their lawless methods of operation disqualified themselves from consideration by a *lawful* court; the Pennsylvania Klansmen, meanwhile, should not bring their grievances to the Federal District Court but should seek redress in state courts empowered with revoking the K.K.K. Pennsylvania charter.

The judge's decision was spelled out in language that left no doubt about his opinion of the Klan and its membership. The scathing indictment is reprinted at considerable length here because it stands as perhaps the most significant condemnation—and accurate description of K.K.K. *modus operandi* during the organization's period of supreme power:

[I find that the Ku Klux Klan has] established and is maintaining a form of despotic rule, which is being operated in secret under the direct sanction and authority of the plaintiff's [Evans'] chief officers; that, in violation of the rights and liberties of the people, it has set up tribunals not known to law, before which citizens of the Commonwealth, not members of the Klan are brought, subjected to some form of trial, and, upon conviction, severe corporal punishments are imposed, painful, humiliating and often brutal in their character, and in some instances destructive of life itself.

[I also find] that in the secret operations of the corporation's activities and in hostility to the civil authorities, military organizations are established and maintained with arms, regalia and equipment, with officers of varying rank and military titles, these officers being bound to obey without question the commands of the superior officer in authority of the plaintiff corporation [K.K.K.]. In addition to this, bands known as "night-riders," or "the black-robed gang," armed, equipped and masked, are formed and operated here and there throughout the country, both organizations being used as instruments of terror, oppression and violence, and being thus a continued menace to the public peace and destructive of the public order.

[I also find] as a fact that Hiram Wesley Evans was present and spoke to the assembled multitude at Carnegie immediately before the riot; that he and Rich were well aware that the civil authorities of Carnegie had forbidden the parade, and that in defiance of this position and in utter disregard of the consequences which might naturally follow, he gave the order to march, which resulted in the serious riot in which men were beaten and severely injured. At least one other man was wounded by gunfire and another man was shot to death. Under these circumstances, he [Evans] was directly responsible for the riot and bloodshed which ensued.

The evidence also disclosed that in the State of Texas men were brought before the Klan, tried and convicted. And in some instances were subjected to brutal beatings and in others were condemned to death and burned at the stake.

In view of all the facts disclosed by the evidence, the plaintiff corporation [K.K.K.], stigmatized as it is by its unlawful acts and conduct, could hardly hope for judicial assistance in a court of the United States which is commissioned to extend to all litigants before it, without distinction of race, creed, color or condition, those high guarantees of liberty and equality vouchsafed by the Constitution of the United States.

This unlawful organization, so destructive of the rights and liberties of the people, has come in vain asking this court of equity for injunction or other relief. They come with filthy hands and can get no assistance here.

After Judge Thomson's decision smashed the Klan's main body of troops, Maine's fiery Democratic leader, W. R. Pattangall—who had led the National

Convention floor fight to condemn the Klan by name
—launched a mop-up campaign. In *The Forum* and
other national magazines, he lashed out at the K.K.K.
with a series of articles that laid bare the Klansmen's
false claims to Americanism. The Klan, he pointed out,
had "caused a tremendous development of anti-Catholic, anti-Jewish and anti-alien sentiment all over the
country" until it had finally become "the rallying point
for all religious and race prejudice in the [nation]"; but,
despite its pious pronouncements of patriotism, the Klan
had done absolutely nothing to further the aims or
better the fortunes of the people of the United States—
even the White Anglo-Saxon Protestants among them
(of which he, himself, was one).

"The one thing the Klan has accomplished so far,"
he wrote, *"has been the enrichment in money and power
of certain persons who, before it was organized, had
neither."*

Pattangall's thorough mop-up of the Klan accomplished what remained to be done after the NVA's original bombardment and Judge Thomson's subsequent
assault. By 1929, K.K.K. membership had shrunk to
82,602. Alabama Senator J. Thomas Heflin, speaking
at a rally of 6,000 recalcitrant Kluxers in New Jersey,
was showered with tomatoes and rotten heads of lettuce
as he left his hotel—and, a few days later, was condemned on the floor of the Senate by a number of his
colleagues, including a fellow southerner, Senator
Bruce Robinson of Arkansas. A group of 1,000 white-
robed and hooded Kluxers, accompanied by 400 members of the K.K.K. Ladies' Auxiliary, attempted to stage
a Memorial Day parade at Jamaica, N.Y.—and were
chased off the streets by a regiment of irate, baseball-
bat-wielding parents. A Texas Klansman, venturing
forth alone in hood and mask on Hallowe'en Night,
was promptly arrested for violating the state's anti-mask
statute and was tossed in jail.

In 1930, Klan membership dropped to 34,694. Imperial Wizard Evans was forced to issue an edict out-

lawing the wearing of a mask or visor with K.K.K. regalia. The old days of terrorist night rides were over; not only had the Klan ceased to be a political power, but, now it had also been shorn of its prime persuasive equipment—anonymity. To remove completely the stigma of the "old" Klan, Evans even changed the name—and those Kluxers who still stayed with him became Knights of the Great Forest. It was all over now —even the shouting. The once-powerful Klan had declined and fallen.

6

K.K.K. IN EXILE

"You will see Yankee bayonets trying to force social equality between the black and white races . . . If that happens, there are those among you who will see blood flow in these streets. The Klan will not permit the people of this country to become a mongrel race."

GRAND DRAGON SAMUEL GREEN,
Wrightsville, Ga., 1948

IT IS FAIRLY EASY to kill a man. It is not much more difficult to kill an army of men. But, as has been proved by the Christian martyrs and the French revolutionaries—and as is being proved today by the Nationalist Chinese and the anti-Castro Cubans—, it is virtually impossible to kill an idea. Unfortunately, this is true of "bad" ideas as well as of good ones; and, though the Ku Klux Klan of the 1920s had been very thoroughly killed, its fallacious ideas of native-born White Anglo-Saxon Protestant supremacy live on.

During the early and mid-1930s, the Klan was rarely heard from as such, but voices of Klan-style bigotry continued to be heard throughout the land. Alabama's racist Senator Thomas J. Heflin continued to deliver heated tirades on the Senate floor against Jews, Negroes and especially Catholics—whom, in as splendid an example of foot-in-mouth disease as history ever recorded, he branded as "the most narrow-minded, intolerant, bigoted people in the United States." George E. Deatherage reorganized the pre-Civil War Knights of the White Camellia and proceeded to declare war on "Jewish Communism." And the "Reverend" Gerald B. Winrod (his "Doctor of Divinity" degree was an "honorary" one, bestowed by the "California Baptist Seminary") set out to "expose" in his monthly magazine, *The Defender,* the Catholic Church as "the harlot of the Bible" and the Jesuit order as "the secret service department of the Pope." (Winrod, interestingly enough, approved of the Nazi extermination of the Jews and criticized Chicago Roman Catholic Cardinal Mundelein for "irreverently" characterizing Adolph Hitler as "an Austrian paperhanger and a poor one at that.")

Overt acts of racial violence had slacked off during this period—but, like the corresponding verbal violence, they had not disappeared entirely. Two particularly brutal incidents merit verbatim reportage here:

> PRINCESS ANNE, Md., October 18, 1933—In the wildest lynching orgy the State has ever witnessed, a frenzied mob of 3,000 men, women and children, sneering at guns and tear gas, overpowered 50 state troopers, tore from a prison cell a negro prisoner accused of attacking an aged white woman, and lynched him in front of the home of a judge who had tried to calm them.

The mob cut down the body, dragged it through the main thoroughfare for more than half a mile, and tossed it onto a burning pyre. Fifty State policemen and deputies battled vainly with the crowd, tossing tear-gas bombs in an effort to disperse it. Five policemen were beaten to the ground and the others were swept aside by the fury of townsmen and farmers, who used a heavy wooden battering ram to smash three doors and reach the cell of the terrified prisoner, George Armwood, 24 years old.

The march to the scene of the lynching was wild in the extreme. The mob members seemed crazed, continually leaping on the negro. Despite the presence of women and children, his clothes were torn from his body and he was hanged nude. One boy, about 18 years old, slashed off the negro's ear with a knife.

—(Reported in *The New York Times*, October 19, 1933)

*   *   *

MARIANNA, Fla., October 27, 1934—The body of Claude Neal, 23, negro, confessed attacker and slayer of a white girl, swung from a tree on the courthouse lawn here victim of an enraged mob's vengeance.

A crowd of 100 men, women and children silently gazed at the body, nude except for a sack reaching from waist to knee. The negro had been shot at least 50 times, burned with red hot irons and dragged through the streets behind an automobile.

An eye-witness . . . gave the following account of the event, which took place in a swamp beside the Chattahoochee River:

"First they cut off his penis. He was made to eat it. Then they cut off his testicles and made him eat them and say he liked it.

"Then they sliced his sides and stomach with knives and every now and then somebody would cut off a finger or toe. Red hot irons were used on the nigger to burn him from top to bottom. From time to time during the torture a rope would be tied around Neal's neck and he was pulled up over a limb and held there until he almost choked to death, when he would be let down and the torture begun all over again. After several hours of this punishment, they decided just to kill him.

"A woman related to the murdered girl drove a butcher knife into Neal's heart. Then the crowd came by and some kicked him and some drove their cars over him."

What remained of the body was brought by the mob to Marianna where it now hangs from a tree on the northeast corner of the courthouse square.

Photographers say they will soon have pictures of the body for sale at fifty cents each. Fingers and toes from Neal's body are being exhibited on street corners.

—(Reported in *The Birmingham Post,* October 27, 1934)

*   *   *

Following the disclosure in 1937 of Hugo L. Black's Klan affiliations (and his subsequent appointment to the U. S. Supreme Court), a new rash of activities broke out involving persons who identified themselves as Klansmen. In September of 1937, a month after Black's appointment, a group of robed Kluxers invited photographers to a meeting at York, Pa. During the same month, an Atlanta Kleagle posed in a warehouse full of Klan regalia—advising photographers that he was shipping the equipment to newly organized Klaverns in various states.

On November 15, 1937, officers of the K.K.K. Miami den—in an unprecedented reversal of traditional procedure—appealed to *police* to close Al Youst's La Paloma Club, the scene of a violent clash between rival Negro bands. Eleven months later, Klansmen burned a cross in the Negro quarter of Lakeland, Fla., after two

Negroes were slain in an all-Negro dance hall; the ceremony, declared the Exalted Cyclops in charge, was "to warn against future disorder."

Incidents such as these seemed to suggest merely that some old die-hard Klansmen were still around—and that they periodically attempted to make themselves heard without being violent or otherwise breaking the law. The truth of the matter—hardly suspected by anyone at the time—was that a huge K.K.K. underground had been established and was now in the process of laying the groundwork for a second full-scale Klan renaissance. The "brains" behind the movement was "Doctor" James A. Colescott, formerly an Indianapolis veterinarian, who had taken over the Knights of the Great Forest when Imperial Wizard Hiram Wesley Evans abdicated.

(After the collapse of the K.K.K., Evans had gone into the asphalt business as a means of augmenting his meager income from the newly formed Grand Forest group. Shortly after that, he had been accused of overcharging the state of Georgia $128,027.13 and had been held by a Federal Court in Atlanta, responsible for treble damages of $384,081.39, plus a $15,000 fine. Subsequently, he had been indicted on charges of conspiring to defraud the state—at which time, he bowed out of the bigotry picture in order to devote full time to saving his own legal skin.)

Operating within the framework of the Great Forest organization, Colescott established skeleton commands in most of the old-time K.K.K. strongholds. "Retired" Grand Dragons were called back into service and enterprising young Kleagles were conscripted to recruit a new rank-and-file membership. The main change in procedure was the scrapping—by Colescott's personal order—of the anti-Catholic attacks and the emphasis instead on the need for "protection" against the "mongrelization" of the "white" race by Negroes and Jews.

The process of establishing new Klan units followed a fairly rigid pattern. First, the newly reactivated Grand Dragon and his Kleagle would visit a community and look up members of the "old" Klan. Under the guise of "just stopping by to say hello," they would determine which of them were interested in getting the "old ball rolling again"—and which had managed to avoid being arrested or otherwise involved in scandal since the last go-round.

Those who were both interested *and* "clean" would be invited to an organizational meeting, at which an Exalted Cyclops and other headquarters personnel were named. Then, an attempt would be made to test the anti-Klan feeling of the area. Small stickers, bearing K.K.K. symbols, would be placed on telephone poles, fences and public buildings. If this tacit declaration of the Klan's presence failed to arouse public furor, other stickers—depicting a masked rider on a rearing horse, and proclaiming: "Knights of the Ku Klux Klan; yesterday, today and forever"—would take their place. If this further manifestation of Klan revival was also met with apathy (or, at least, without *great* opposition), it would be time for the burning of a cross—usually in an open field or somewhere else where no great significance could be attached to the act.

If the community continued to display indifference at this point, it was time for more forceful displays. Crosses would be burned in protest to Negro violence, as in Lakeland, Fla. Klokards would make public speeches denouncing Communism, un-Americanism and "integrationism." Parades featuring robed and masked Klansmen would be peacefully staged. The community, in short, would be advised that the K.K.K. was back in business—but in a form and with a style much less inacceptable than that of the "old" Klan. To keep things under control on a national level, Imperial Wizard Colescott left the Atlanta headquarters of the Klan's government-in-exile and went to Washington, D.C., for a voluntary appearance before Representative Martin Dies' Committee Investigating Un-American Activities. Dies declared that he wanted facts about "every state in which the Ku Klux Klan is operating"; Colescott promptly assured him full cooperation.

Thus, putting forth this new "image" of patriotism

and respect for lawfully constituted authority, the old Invisible Empire began once more to grow—this time, more invisibly than ever. It was not always easy, of course; sometimes, "new school" Klansmen found themselves being assailed by an indignant citizenry that still remembered the "old school" operation. In Charleston, S.C., for example, the State Grand Dragon staged an open-air rally on July 4, 1941—and an audience of 3,000 booed him, hissed him and finally drove him out of the city with a barrage of overripe tomatoes and rotten eggs. Also, Grand Dragons in some areas—mindful of the way Imperial Wizards of old had helped themselves to the K.K.K. treasury—refused to become subordinate to the Colescott Klan and formed independent units of their own. In Alabama, a roofing contractor named William Hugh Morris organized the Federated Ku Klux Klans, Inc., and named *himself* Imperial Wizard. In the South Georgia-North Florida-East Alabama area, "Parson" Jack Johnston and Attorney Fred New set up the Original Southern Klans, Inc. And, in Central Florida, a group called Southern Knights of the Ku Klux Klan came into being—with a leader known only as "His Imperial Majesty, Samuel the Second." Before unamused police officers stepped in and broke them up, a group of New Yorkers had also managed to get into the act—with a leader named "Chief of Staff of the Invisible Planet, Knights of the Air." To complete the picture, there were the Knights of the Ku Klux Klan of America, formed at Montgomery, Ala., by an itinerant oddball named "Doctor" Lycurgus Spinks, and the Association of Georgia Klans, an insurrectionary offshoot of Colescott's Invisible Empire, presided over by Atlanta obstetrician, Dr. Samuel Green.

In 1944, Federal and State agents set out after the largest group—Colescott's Invisible Empire—and promptly annihilated it. The procedure was simple: Atlanta Collector of Internal Revenue Marion H. Allen filed a $685,000 tax suit against the concern, alleging that this amount was owed the Government in corporate income taxes. When the Empire failed to come up with the money, the state of Georgia revoked its charter. Colescott dropped out of sight and his members were divided up among other Klans.

Dr. Green, of the Association of Georgia Klans, promptly reorganized his group into an unchartered, voluntary association and sought to do business "as a church"—which would be untaxable. Other leaders followed suit. Their monetary wings clipped thusly, the organizations were unable to make any bid for great political power. But, they still had recourse to other avenues of attack—and, as months passed, they explored them more and more thoroughly.

*　　*　　*

On June 3, 1946, a cross was burned in front of a Jewish fraternity house at the University of Southern California. The following night, another was burned in front of the home of a Los Angeles Negro physician. Before the week was over, Hollywood's Temple Israel had been ravaged by unknown vandals; swastikas and hate slogans had been painted in black across its walls; Rabbi Max Nussbaum, a refugee from Nazi Germany, had received obscene and threatening phone calls.

In Detroit, more than 1,200 white-robed pickets patrolled Sojourner Truth Homes, a government-backed project of that city's housing commission; many were armed with knives, clubs, rifles and shotguns. They had come to prevent 65 Negro families from moving into the project; two truckloads of furniture belonging to Negroes were destroyed; Negroes who tried to cross the picket line were stoned.

"The wartime shortage of sheets and bigotry was lifting," observed *Time* magazine. "The postwar Ku Klux Klan . . . was on the loose again."

In 1947, after President Harry S. Truman boldly espoused the first Civil Rights legislation since the reconstruction era, fifteen hooded men of "Parson" Jack Johnston's Original Southern Klans, Inc., stormed a Phoenix City, Ala., courtroom and staged a demonstration in the jury box. In Swainsboro, Ga., 189 masked and hooded Klansmen burned a 10-foot cross on the lawn of the Emmanuel County Courthouse; Grand Dragon Green assailed Truman and offered the prophecy that integration wouldn't end "at the bedroom door." Wearing his brightly colored and delicately embroidered robe, he declared: "We rededicate our lives to the protection of white womanhood." Those in his audience who remembered (and, perhaps, still carried with them fears from) Thomas E. Watson's obsessively sexual heyday cackled delightedly.

In Iron City, Ga., robed masked men started across a cow pasture toward the house of Mayor C. L. Drake, an outspoken Klan antagonist. The one-armed mayor peppered them with buckshot and drove them away. They were coming to kidnap him, he told reporters, because of his sharp criticism of Governor Herman Talmadge—not a Klansman himself, but known to be not unsympathetic with K.K.K. members.

In Lakeview, Ga., 18 hooded Kluxers set up a burning cross in front of the house of high school athletic coach Walter Bowland—who had had an argument with a student thought to be the son of one of the Klansmen. Two days later, while the coach was at a basketball game, another pistol-packing band of night-riders came to the house and frightened his pregnant wife. Bowland telephoned Catoosa County Sheriff Jim Moreland, who told him: "I'm just as scared of the Ku Klux Klan as you are."

On March 6, 1948, the eve of the Democratic primaries in Johnson County, Ga., a 249-car cavalcade of hooded, masked and bed-sheet-bedecked Kluxers moved into Wrightsville, where 400 Negroes had registered to vote. As 700 spectators cheered, they set fire to a cross on the courthouse lawn. Grand Dragon Green then mounted the courthouse stairs and delivered a heated tirade against "nigger-lover" Harry Truman.

If Truman's civil rights legislation is carried out, he promised, "you will see Yankee bayonets trying to force social equality between the black and white races . . .

If that happens, there are those among you who will see blood flow in these streets. The Klan will not permit the people of this country to become a mongrel race."

When he finished the speech, his followers dispersed. One report charges, they then made the rounds of Wrightsville's Negroes, threatening, "a vote for Truman is a vote for your own lynching." The report is lent credence by the fact that, of the 400 registered Negroes, not a single one voted the following day.

A week later, on Pine Mountain, Ga., some 500 K.K.K. recruits gathered outside a tar-paper shack to "take the obligation" and become full-fledged members of the order. Among them were three "aliens"—reporters James Bellows, and Carlton Johnson and photographer Joe Talbot, of *The Columbus Ledger*—who had come to write a story about the Klan's biggest gathering in 20 years.

When Grand Dragon Green stepped out of the shack, Talbot started shooting flashbulbs. Immediately, eight burly Klansmen pounced on him and smashed his equipment. Another hooded squad leaped on Johnson and Bellows and carried them into the shack.

Now, a heavy-set Kluxer handed each of the trio a pint of whiskey and commanded: "Drink." When the newspapermen refused, other Klansmen threatened that they would pour the liquor down their throats. They drank—about a pint each in half an hour; Bellows passed out; Johnson and Talbot, half-unconscious, were jabbed with a hypodermic needle.

Next, the three men were carried to their car. Bellows and Johnson were stripped, then put into the back seat—arranged in a position which suggested they were engaged in an act of homosexual intercourse. Klansmen then photographed them with cameras of their own.

Finally, two Kluxers drove the car and its human cargo to the town of Manchester. The steering wheel was wiped clear of fingerprints and the Klansmen vanished. Minutes later, a Manchester cop arrested the newsmen for drunkenness. Their city editor bailed them out—and, the Sunday morning *Ledger-Examiner* spread the story across its front page.

The following day, a cross was burned in front of the *Ledger-Examiner's* offices.

* * *

When November of 1948 rolled around, the Ku Klux Klan was determined to defeat that "son of a bitch of a nigger-lover" in the White House. But it was equally antagonistic toward his opponent, New York Governor Thomas E. Dewey—who, like Truman, believed that Negroes were human beings. As a result, they campaigned vigorously for "Dixiecrat" J. Strom Thurmond, who had bolted his party and tossed his hat into the Presidential ring on the "States' Rights" ticket.

Reports filtered North of an immense intimidation campaign throughout the South. Klansmen paid midnight visits to persons thought to be Truman or Dewey supporters, threatening violent punishment to those who dared venture out to the polls; on election day, unhooded Klansmen patrolled the polling booths to make sure their message got across. When all the votes were in nationally, Truman managed to squeeze out a slim victory; Dewey was second and Thurmond was at the bottom of the heap.

But, the Klan had made itself known; as in the 20s, it was once again interested in politics—and was prepared to break laws to tip the scales of justice in its favor. (In all fairness, it must be acknowledged that U. S. Senator J. Strom Thurmond never—to this author's knowledge—publicly solicited the support of the Klan, nor did he in any way state that such support was welcome; therefore, any similarity between speeches made by him at that time or subsequently and speeches made by Klansmen "states' rights" advocates as detailed herein must be regarded as coincidental.)

There are two more incidents concerning the Klan which, it is felt, should be related at this point. Both are from *Time* magazine, and are reprinted in their entirety.

March 15, 1948—A great many Georgians were intensely displeased by this tawdry barbarism (displayed at a recent K.K.K. Konklave). Governor Melvin Thompson took steps to counteract it. He ordered two prisoners removed from Reidsville's safe Tatnall State Prison and sent back to a rural jail in Emmanuel County where they are accused of having murdered a state patrolman. This was done to prove that no Georgian would lynch them. The Governor said that the Klan meetings should be outlawed. His reason: their activities might encourage the interference of Northern "race baiters."

January 3, 1949—In Talladega, Ala., a white-hooded delegation of Ku Kluxers and a white-bearded Santa Claus presented a radio to Jack Riddle, a 107-year-old Negro, and his wife, Josey, 86, so they could have their wish, to "hear the preachers." Grand Dragon Samuel Green explained that this demonstrated the "heart of a Klansman," called in photographers to take the most incongruous picture of the week—(two chair-borne Negroes, a white-bearded Santa and 15 masked-hooded-and-robed Klansmen).

In retrospect, the decade from 1940 to 1950 seems to have been the Kluxers' un-finest hour. Much of the time, their confused meanderings resembled those of the Keystone Cops. Beset by lawsuits, hounded by Federal tax collectors and pillaged by the newspapers (even in the South), they never really managed to exert any significant influence, nor to display any significant power. During the decade that was to come, the well-laid organizational plans of Imperial Wizard Colescott would pay dividends—and the K.K.K. would once again become something of a power. But, for the time being, the state of the Klan was a sorry state indeed. Perhaps, it is therefore altogether fitting and proper that the farcical decade should come to a close with the most farcical event in the Klan's history—the nationwide press conference of Imperial Emperor Lycurgus Spinks.

7

THE IMPERIAL EMPEROR MEETS THE PRESS

> *"There's a million of them now and in five years there'll be five million. If you ain't one of them, you won't know who they are and you won't know where they are. You'll just know they are there, and there ain't no power on earth can stop them."*
>
> IMPERIAL EMPEROR LYCURGUS SPINKS,
> Washington, D. C., 1949

COMPARED WITH most leaders of the Klan, the Sphinx of Egypt is as talkative as a rock 'n' roll disc jockey. Indeed, the late Grand Dragon of the Georgia K.K.K., Dr. Samuel Green, often remained *so* silent for *so* long a time that *Atlanta Constitution* editor Ralph McGill called him "the Reluctant Dragon."

A significant exception to this policy of "Practice, Don't Preach" was Lycurgus Spinks (pronounced "sphinx"), self-appointed Imperial Emperor of the Knights of the Ku Klux Klan of America—in other words, "boss-man" of the whole menagerie. Spinks was so talkative that newsmen began referring to him as "the victim of a severe case of verbal diarrhea."

Born on a plantation near Thomasville, Ala., where he was "raised by a nigger mammy" and ate "potlicker out of the same bowl with the pickaninnies," the Imperial Emperor spent his early manhood touring the South as an unordained Baptist minister. For almost ten years he filled pastorates in Arkansas and the Carolinas—leaving one post and moving to another when his qualifications (or lack of them) were questioned by suspicious congregations.

Eventually, he tired of preaching "the Word" and began delivering "For Men Only" and "For Women Only" lectures on sexology. His academic credentials for this chore remained as mysterious as his ministerial qualifications, but he took the liberty of calling himself "Doctor" Spinks and roared his Elmer Gantry-like orations at eager audiences that sometimes numbered well into the thousands.

Once, pinned down by a reporter's questions, he admitted that "no college ever gave me that title [of doctor]."

Where, then, did he obtain it?

"I just been known as 'Doctor' Spinks nearly ever since I could remember," he explained.

Soon, he also grew weary of his role as sexual missionary. He then began touring the South with a series of lectures for which he billed himself as "The Reincarnation of George Washington."

As Washington Reincarnate, Spinks whipped the "hill-people" into a frenzy of superpatriotism. It was not uncommon, on better nights, to find his audiences kissing the American flag and singing "The Star Spangled Banner" as they marched out of the lecture tent. If any of those present recognized him as a one-time wandering sexologist, it didn't seem to bother them.

Spinks would usually begin an address with what he called a "joke." A typical example went something like this:

"What was the first pin a master Mason ever wore?"

"A *safety* pin. Ha-ha-ha!"

He would then make a transition to the Reconstruction era and fill the air with bitter denunciations of the "carpet-baggers," "Yankees," "do-gooders" and other "enemies of the South."

Sipping diluted apple cider as he went along, he would proceed to pile up "evidence" against the Federal Government's "wanton invasion" of states' rights. Then, he would move deftly to the subject of Negro demands for equality.

The "good nigger," he would point out, is "happy" to occupy a secondary place in society; it is only when "agitatin' Jews" and other "Yankee profiteers" come South and "fill his head with nonsense" that he "begins to act uppity."

The solution to the problem, he would say, was pure and simple: Show "the no-good Jew bastards" that the South "wouldn't stand for" the infiltration tactics of those who would "corrupt our niggers."

At times, to make his point more forcefully, he would jerk off his coat, roll up his shirtsleeves and display his flexed biceps. *That,* he would tell the frenzied mob, was how *he'd* handle any "uppity nigger" that sat down next to *him* at a lunch counter.

It wasn't long after the start of this "superpatriotism" lecture series that Spinks stepped out of the role of Washington Reincarnate and into the role of Imperial Emperor of the Knights of the Ku Klux Klan of America. He promptly announced that his organization had 265,000 members in six states—and was still growing.

"They are scattered from Yaller Rabbit to Vinegar Bend," he declared. "They go under all sorts of names. Some of them—like the 'Knights of Liberty' and 'The Seventy-Sixers'—don't even have the word Klan in their title. But they ain't a thing but old Ku Kluxes. This nation's full of the blame things. They're everywhere. There's the Seashores and the Ozarks and the Lone Stars and the Independents and the Allieds and the River Vallies and the I-don't-know-what-all else. All I need is some good men to go out and bring 'em all into the fold."

The arrival on the Klan scene of the verbose little man with the amusingly redundant title of Imperial

Emperor came as something of a surprise to many of the older, established K.K.K. leaders—who were rather annoyed by his speeches and rather incredulous of his claims. From a jail cell at Birmingham, Ala.—where he was doing time for refusing to turn over his membership records to a grand jury—Imperial Wizard William Hugh Morris, head of the Federated Ku Klux Klans, Inc., said he had never heard of Spinks until the lecturer breezed into Birmingham one morning and offered to make speeches that would get him out of "the can."

"I told him to go ahead and talk if he wanted to," Morris recalled. "I figured he couldn't do any harm, and I was willing to do anything that would help put my feet on the ground. He went out and talked to a couple of Klans of mine, and the first thing I knew he was down there at Montgomery calling himself 'Emperor' and claiming to be the head of something called the Knights of the Ku Klux Klan of America. Two hundred and sixty-five thousand members, my foot! If he's got 25 men paying dues, it will surprise me."

Spinks replied to Morris' slur with good humor. If the jailed Klan chief was any kind of a leader, he said, he wouldn't be in jail—now, would he? And, if a man makes deprecating remarks about someone who's doing a better job than he is, that sounds a little bit like professional jealousy—now, doesn't it?

Having rebutted "the competition," the Imperial Emperor launched another campaign to increase the number of his followers. Before long, he was claiming a total national membership half the population of the state of Mississippi and predicting that his "flock" would quintuple within the next five years.

Spink-allied Klansmen, he declared flatly, were *everywhere*—"if you ain't one of them, you won't know who they are and you won't know where they are! You'll just know that they are there, and there ain't no power on earth can stop 'em."

So great was the Emperor's confidence in the omnipresence of his "empire" that he began making speeches as far north as New York—and, when he was invited to appear on the popular radio program, "Meet the

Press," he graciously responded that he'd be "dee-lighted."

The nationally broadcast confrontation took place in the autumn of 1949, presented by the Mutual Broadcasting System in association with the editors of *The American Mercury* magazine. On the "Meet the Press" panel were columnist and commentator Drew Pearson, who had exposed the activities of a number of Klan units throughout the South; Lawrence E. Spivak, then the editor of *The American Mercury* (presently a permanent panelist on NBC-TV's version of "Meet the Press"); Edward T. Folliard, of *The Washington Post* (now that newspaper's White House correspondent), and May Craig, of the Portland, Me., *Press-Herald,* one of the outstanding female journalists of the decade. Moderator of the panel was Albert Warner, of the Mutual network.

Before beginning the general questioning, moderator Warner asked Spinks if he cared to make an opening statement.

The Imperial Emperor replied:

"I'm fully conscious of the fact that every newsman that I'm facing tonight is an arch-enemy of the organization that I represent. I naturally presume that you hate me because I'm a Klansman. And now, as soon as I say hello to the finest grand-baby on earth, I'll be ready to start battling with you. Hello, little son. Stay in there and pitch for your grand-daddy. I'm going to make him a Klansman at 10 years old."

Mrs. Craig took exception to the hostile attitude toward the panel.

"Newspaper people don't hate anybody," she said. "We just try to find out what makes them tick."

The Imperial Emperor chose not to debate the point with her. She then asked him how many "subjects" he had in his empire.

"I wouldn't tell you that if I knew," he replied.

"Why? Is it a secret?"

"Yes, ma'am."

"Why a secret in a democratic country?"

"Because it's expedient to have secrecy in a democratic country."

"A secret organization in a democratic country? Do you . . . feel that the Klan is above the law? Is that why you keep it a secret?"

"Certainly not. It's the one organization in America today that has the grace and the grits and the backbone to stand up four-square and defy all people who propose to destroy our laws and our Constitution and our Government—particularly the Communists of this country."

The American Mercury editor, Spivak, found it difficult to reconcile this statement with the Klan's reputation as a terrorist group.

"Do you think that flogging, terrorizing and lynching —all of which the Klan has been accused of—create a respect for law?" he asked.

"There has never been a Klan in this United States that ever endorsed flogging or in any way violating the law," replied Spinks. "Every Klansman in this country takes an oath to this effect—that he will obey the law himself and that he will under all circumstances aid and assist all constituted officers of the law in the faithful performance of their legal duty."

"Are you suggesting," pressed Spivak, "that there have been no night-riders, that there have been no floggings on the part of Klansmen?"

Spinks quickly back-peddled.

"I would not say that no Klansman ever flogged anybody," he said. "But we had a *Klansman* down in Alabama the other night that got flogged (himself) . . . I don't know who flogged him. It certainly wasn't another Klansman."

Spivak failed to be convinced.

"But doesn't the very secrecy of your organization encourage that kind of lawlessness?" he asked.

"No, sir!" replied Spinks.

"Isn't the purpose of your organization to control and keep down the Negroes?" asked May Craig. "Isn't that your prime purpose?"

"No, sir!" Spinks told her. "One of the purposes of

our organization is to see that the Negroes in the United States get a square deal at the hands of white people and everybody else that has to do with the laws in this country."

"Then why," she demanded, "are all Negroes and all Negro organizations against you?"

"They are not against us."

"Name one that is for you," said Edward Folliard.

"All the niggers down South know that the best friend they've got on earth is the Knights of the Ku Klux Klan."

"Could you name some organization that has endorsed the Klan?" Folliard pressed. "Some Negro organization?"

Spinks seemed to think about it for a moment. Finally, he replied:

"I don't keep up with Negro organizations except what the Baptist Church is doing among niggers. That's the only one I've preached in."

"Well," interrupted editor Spivak, "if you have such a wonderful organization, and the Negroes and all the white people in the South are for you, why must you hide behind masks as you've done all these years? Why must you keep your membership secret?"

"We do not have to hide behind a mask. I stated to you that the first official act of my administration was to command all Klansmen in the Invisible Empire to remove their masks."

[Actually, the Klan in Alabama was unmasked by State law. But the Imperial Emperor, unlike other Klan leaders, "endorsed" the law—and said that he would persuade his "subjects" to observe it. "Son," he told a reporter, "by the time I get through talking to 'em, they'll be so proud to be a Klansman that they'll walk out there with their faces as bare as a baby's behind."]

Spivak acknowledged that the Klan had been unmasked, but asked why they wore masks in public *before* the legal unmasking.

"What were they afraid of?" he demanded.

"Not a thing in the world," said Spinks.

"Every self-respecting organization that I know of,

that does a patriotic job, always wants its face to be seen," Spivak continued. "Why did the Klansmen hide theirs? And why do you hide from each other now?"

"We do not hide from each other," Spinks replied angrily. "We do not hide from the public. Our faces are wide open. In all our parades now, you can see the boys face to face. And if it's expedient and necessary for any Klansman to keep his membership secret, then it's his business to stay out of the parade."

Spivak decided not to pursue the line of questioning any further. Then Drew Pearson, who to this point had been watching with an "I-expected-as-much" expression of vexation, tried to pin down Spinks on the extent of his "domain."

"Emperor," he asked, "do you represent the Georgia Klans?"

"I represent the Knights of the Ku Klux Klan of America, all of them," said Spinks.

"Do you represent the Federated Klans?"

"Every Klansman in America."

"They claim you don't."

Spinks' face turned red. His fist clenched, he scowled at Pearson and shouted angrily:

"I'm here to speak for them and defend them in any attack that you make—and I'd like for you to start making them, old man. Every criticism that you ever made of the Knights of the Ku Klux Klan on your program has been—not—not one single word of truth in it."

"And now, Emperor . . ." Pearson began.

"And," Spinks roared on, ignoring the attempted interruption, "this spy that you've got down in—in one of our Klans in Atlanta—is a *moral degenerate,* a leper, and every time you quote him over the radio you are aiding and assisting a man who has repudiated one of the most sacred oaths that a man ever took."

[The reference was to a member of a Georgia Klan, unidentified by name, who was believed by Spinks to have tipped off Pearson on a number of Klan terror-sprees. According to the Imperial Emperor, a non-Klansman—or an "alien," as K.K.K. terminology brands the "uninitiated"—cannot be expected to comprehend the "noble" aims of the order, and thus may be forgiven for antagonistic attitudes; but a member who has taken the Klan oath and then "conspires with the enemy" is beneath contempt. In one particularly fiery speech before his Alabama Klan, Spinks branded such conspirators as "despicable and contemptible degenerates" and threatened that, if he caught any member of his organization acting as a "spy," he would pierce his ears and hang from each ear a ring marked "traitor."]

Pearson waited silently for the tirade to end. Then he resumed his questioning.

"You were once Grand Dragon of the Mississippi Klans?" he asked.

"Yes," replied Spinks.

"They claim down there that you were not."

"Well, I don't care what they claim. They're just like you. They claim anything on the earth that pays off politically or financially."

"That includes Governor Fielding Wright, I suppose?"

"It certainly does."

"You once sued him for $50,000 . . ."

"I certainly did."

". . . because he disclaimed you."

"No, sir. That's not true."

"How did the suit come about?"

"I sued him because he threw a—a slanderous dagger into my back, in my absence, at night, after the sun went down over Arkansas. I withdrew the $50,000 suit against him without prejudice. And, remember this, brother—and I hope the Governor is listening: That suit's renewal depends entirely on his conduct from here on out."

Pearson yielded the floor to Spivak, who asked:

"Do you think lynching is ever justified?"

"No," said Spinks.

"Do you think that cross-burning is ever justified?"

"Yes—if you want to burn one."

"Well, you're a Baptist Minister . . ."

"I'm an *American*," thundered Spinks, "and a free-born one, and if I want to burn a cross I'll set it afire. If you can put it out, just come on."

"The Baptist Church Organization in the South has denounced the Klan and the Klansman's creed as un-Christian," said Spivak. "They say the cross must be *borne,* not burned. How do you, as a Baptist Minister, condone the burning of the cross?"

Spinks' "explanation" was as follows:

"The Knights of the Ku Klux Klan believes and practices and preaches and proposes to die for everything that Baptists believe. There's 238 communistic organizations in the United States that say everything Baptists believe and preach is a lie. Why don't they take a shot at *them?*"

"But, Dr. Spinks . . ." Spivak began.

"They haven't got the guts," Spinks said, answering his own question.

Spivak tried a new tack.

"Do you, as a Baptist minister, believe that the cross should be burned or borne?" he asked.

"Both," said the Imperial Emperor. Then, he added: "How you going to *borne* a cross? Who ever heard of such a fool thing?"

"That's what Jesus said," May Craig advised him.

"Jesus never said any such thing," snapped Spinks.

"Do you believe that Jesus would have been a Klansman if He were alive?" Spivak asked.

"I believe He *was.*"

At this point, Edward Folliard resumed questioning about Klan brutality and night-riding.

"Emperor," he said, "in Georgia and Alabama, 30 Klansmen have been indicted for outrages. Do you disavow those 30 men?"

"Where do you get your information?" Spinks parried.

"In a very reputable newspaper, *The New York Times.*"

"Well, they don't know what they're talking about. I'll give you the facts if you want them."

"Have any of your members been indicted?"

"They claim that three out of 18 are Klansmen. One of them talked to me about it and told me that he was in Florida on his vacation when the flogging that they accused him of took place, and he could prove it by a hundred witnesses. I begged the courts in Birmingham to try these men they indicted six or eight weeks ago, begged them like a dog to try them. They've got more judges in Birmingham than they have fiddlers in Hell, but you can't get them to try them . . . You know why? They're scared to do it. They're afraid the whole thing will wash out . . ."

"Isn't it a fact that your organization has lost greatly in numbers? Isn't it much weaker than it was?"

"Certainly. A great many of them died. We had two-and-a-half million in 1923 and '24 and '25, and now we've got only about a million. A great many of them died. And it's an underground organization. It was born in a cave, and when it's necessary to get out of the way of our enemies, we duck and go under the ground. We had to do it fifteen years ago. When this New Deal crowd (a reference to the administration of President Franklin D. Roosevelt, who was unsympathetic with the "superpatriot" aims of the Klan) started to cut our throats, we just went underground and told them where to go. I don't know whether they went or not."

There followed then an exchange between Pearson and Spinks that sounded almost as if it had been written by one of Fred Allen's comedy writers.

"Emperor," said the columnist, "you once posed as the reincarnation of George Washington."

"I did," said Spinks, ". . . and I made a good job of it."

"Which did you find more lucrative—posing as George Washington or running the Ku Klux Klan?"

"Well, I haven't tried running the Klan long enough to give you that answer . . ."

"Do you think George Washington would have stood for floggings at night, and secret raids, and the beatings and the carryings on that your . . ."

"No, and the Ku Klux Klan of America has never endorsed it either. And I challenge you and tell you that there's not a word of truth in that assumption."

Spivak interjected a question about the membership

of the Klan and Spinks refused to say if any Senators or Congressmen were on the rolls.

"Why not?" asked Spivak.

"Because I don't want to," replied the Imperial Emperor.

"That's because you don't know, isn't it?" demanded Pearson.

"Well, I wouldn't say I don't know," said Spinks.

"Isn't it the truth," pressed Pearson, "that you've been in this game a very short time, and that you don't even know who's under you?"

"I don't think it's a fair question at all," replied Spinks. Accordingly, he refused to answer.

May Craig then attempted to persuade Spinks to spell out the "brotherhood" policies of the Klan.

"As a Baptist minister and a clergyman," she said, "you must regard all men as brothers. Do you regard Jews, Catholics and Negroes as your brothers?"

"I most assuredly do," he replied. "That is, I believe in the universal Fatherhood of God. I'm a brother of all of them."

"Then why do you not allow them in your organization?"

"Listen. They can come in the very minute that they qualify."

"You mean a Negro must say he's not a Negro?"

"Well, he couldn't join, because it's a white man's organization."

"That's what I mean."

"All right. A Jew can't join because he denies the virgin birth of Christ. A Catholic can't join because he has allegiance to the Pope of Rome, and no man can be a Klansman who has allegiance outside of the United States . . . Some of the best friends on earth I've got are Jews and Catholics, and we discuss things pro and con right out of the heart. We never have any differences about it. If they could become Klansmen, I'd be tickled to death for them to do it. But they just haven't got what it takes . . . You've got to be a white, native-born, gentile Protestant to join the Klan. Now, that ought to answer all that."

"How," asked Spivak, "do you reconcile all that with Americanism?"

Said Spinks:

"It [the Klan] stands for constitutional government; it stands for the enforcement of law; it stands for free enterprise; it stands for our American way of life . . . We might just as well get down to the milk in the cocoa-nut: Everybody in America who has sense enough to know whether John the Baptist ate wild honey or salt or molasses knows that the Communists in this country and their activities are the greatest threat to American liberty and freedom that this nation ever saw. And we, the Klansmen of this country, are not going to take it lying flat on our backs."

Pearson seized upon the Imperial Emperor's claims of "Americanism" to direct a series of *ad hominem* questions that illuminated much of Spinks' past. The exchange was so tragi-comic that it deserves to be re-produced in full:

PEARSON: You've been posing here as a great American. Now, you were once a preacher, a Baptist preacher . . .

SPINKS: I am now.

P: All right. You say you still are. I doubt that; but, anyway, you preached at Blacksburg, South Carolina. Why did you leave there, and what happened?

S: Why I left Blacksburg, South Carolina? Because I went to—you want to make this thing personal?

P: No. You're . . .

S: You want to run this thing into personalities?

P: You're—you're posing as a great American . . .

S: I'm posing as it and I *am!*

P: All right. Then tell us why you left Blacksburg.

S: Because I wanted to move to Mississippi to my plantation.

P: And didn't South Carolina try to extradite you from Mississippi?

S. No. That's a lie.

P: Well now, weren't you a receiver for a bank in Blacksburg?

S: Yes.

P: And weren't the accounts found to be out of order?

S: No.

P: They tell me exactly the opposite.

S: All right.

P: You remember J. H. Bridges and J. H. Allison in Blacksburg?

S: Yes.

P: They preferred charges against you on behalf of the stockholders of the bank.

S: All right. Go ahead.

P: And Governor Bilbo of Mississippi refused to extradite.

S: No. He was never asked to do it.

P: Well, your denial is not good enough for me.

S: Well, my denial is certainly . . .

P: I was—I was on the telephone to Blacksburg about 35 minutes ago . . .

S: Bilbo is dead.

P: . . . and they tell me exactly the opposite.

S: You can't do anything about it. Bilbo is dead. But I've been in South Carolina numbers of times, and spoken. I held a meeting in South Carolina in—in the capital since then.

P: Because the statute of limitations has run out.

S: No. There is no statute of limitations. I say that these fellows you're talking about got sore with me because I wouldn't let them rob the poor. They were stockholders—robbing the poor people who had their money in that bank, to send their children to school with.

P: You say you're a Baptist minister. I have a letter here from the secretary-treasurer of the Baptist Church of South Carolina who says you are not.

S: Well, he's a liar.

May Craig, at this point, took up the questioning. "Will you tell me, please, what is your salary?" she asked. "How much money do you make out of the job? Do you have any other jobs?"

"That certainly is nobody's business but mine," replied Spinks.

"Why would you object to saying, when you hold a more-or-less public office?" she demanded.

"Well," said Spinks, "I've only been in (office) about two weeks. Give me a little time. See how much I can make out of it!"

Moderator Warner returned to the subject of the Klan and its Americanism.

"Does it [the Klan] stand, for example, for voting by Negroes?" he asked.

"You mean . . . nigger voting?" replied Spinks.

"Uh—let's call them—let's call them Negroes," said Warner.

"Yes," said Spinks, "I want Negroes to vote. We call them Negroes and I call them brother in the Baptist Church."

"Do you not prevent them from voting?" asked May Craig.

"No," said Spinks. "I'm in favor of them voting."

"Negroes report that you prevent them," she insisted.

"They do not . . ."

"Yes, sir. Your Klan stands around . . ."

"Well, I wouldn't know about that."

" . . . at the polls."

"Never heard of it in my life."

"You need to look around, don't you?"

"Listen," said Spinks angrily, "when the Klans were organized in 1866, all the white men in the South were disenfranchised. And the only way that they could get their government back and re-establish a white man's government was to kill the dog-gone carpet-baggers and put the niggers back to work, and they did it that way!"

Finally, the panel returned to the subject of the Klan's penchant for secrecy—as evidenced by the wearing of masks.

"Emperor," asked Edward Folliard, "why did the State of Alabama enact a law unmasking the Klan?"

"Because," replied Spinks, "the politicians figured that the Klan wasn't strong enough in that state to re-elect them. And now, in about four months from now, they'll want to repeal the infernal thing, so they can get the Klan to vote for them. That's what they did it for."

"Why is it," asked Spivak, "if your organization is an American organization, that so many states have tried to outlaw the Ku Klux Klan?"

"I don't know that they done it," said the Imperial Emperor. "But how do I know why a state will do a thing? It depends on its leadership."

"Well," pressed Spivak, "they haven't tried to outlaw any of the other organizations, the Roman Catholic organizations, the Jewish organizations."

"There's 238 Communist organizations in this country," replied Spinks, with questionable relevancy, "and we can't get anybody to outlaw *them!*"

"The Klansmen," said Spivak, "have invariably denied the responsibility for acts of mob violence, haven't they?"

"Yes."

"Doesn't the very existence of a secret organization such as yours, with masks and hoods and the rest of it, give irresponsibile people a shield behind which to break the law?"

"I wouldn't say that."

"Well, hasn't the law been broken by such people? You admitted that a minute ago."

"Well, now we've taken the masks off."

"Well, why don't you take the secrecy out now too?"

"I'm not a-going to take the secrecy out of it. Jesus Christ taught the expedience of secrecy when He asked the Apostle Peter who He was and he told Him; He said, well, don't tell anybody; keep your mouth shut until I get into Jerusalem and get this job done."

And thus, having met the press with generous servings of preachment, patriotism and paranoia, the Imperial Emperor of the Knights of the Ku Klux Klan of America went his way — presumably, like Christ, to "get this job done."

8

SECOND COMEBACK

"People in other parts of the country like to think of niggers as human beings because they have hands and feet. So do apes and gorillas have hands and feet. If a nigger has a soul, I never read about it in the Bible. The only good nigger is a dead nigger."

—HORACE MAITTON,
Jacksonville, Fla., 1958

THE KU KLUX KLAN, W. R. Pattangall observed in 1925, is more than just an organization; it is a state of mind. The truth of this observation was never more apparent than during the decade from 1950 to 1960. The K.K.K. was disorganized; its coffers were bare; its membership was scattered among some two dozen "independent" units; its "leadership" resembled the rejects from the casting call of a Mack Sennett comedy. And yet, though bound only by a broad unity of purpose, the Kluxers swept across the South in a wave of violence and terror unsurpassed since the riotous days of the original Invisible Empire.

In February of 1951, a band of 50 rifle- and shot-gun-wielding night marauders stormed the Columbia County, North Carolina, home of 38-year-old Mrs. Evergreen Flowers. After firing some several hundred bullets through the windows of the house, they busted down the door and chased Mrs. Flowers' husband away. Then, they dragged the woman outside, tied her legs with plow lines, stripped her, gagged her with her own undergarments and beat her into unconsciousness with sticks, baseball bats and gun butts. The reason for the vicious assault: Mrs. Flowers, a Negro, had been "running around with white men."

Before the month was over, the same Klansmen had dragged two other Negroes and ten Caucasians from their Columbus County homes and flogged them. The reasons cited for the outrages were that the victims had been "guilty" of "cursing near women," "not attending church regularly" or "drinking too much."

In Dora, Ala., a group of 100 Kluxers raided the home of Mrs. Irene Burton, 38. The woman—a Caucasian—was stripped naked and viciously whipped with a length of hemp. Her 16-year-old daughter, Sally, was forced to watch—with a noose tied around her neck.

In Mobile, Ala., during a single month, a Negro home and elementary school were burned, three other Negro homes were bombed, a group of Negro schoolchildren were stoned and 20 public cross burnings were celebrated. Mobile Police Chief Dudley E. McFayden held a special meeting of his entire department and threatened to cancel days off unless the violence was halted. "I would like to ask one question," he said. "Why has there been no arrest? Several crosses were burned in the same territory. Another question: Where were the police?" Later, he told reporters that 40 percent of Mobile's terror had been traced directly to the Klan and that he had placed an undercover agent inside a Klan Konklave. There were arrests, but the violence continued; it is impossible to arrest a "state of mind."

When, on May 17, 1954, the U. S. Supreme Court outlawed segregation in public schools, the K.K.K. gained *real* impetus. In Wildwood, Fla., a gang of hooded terrorists dragged Negro Jesse Woods from his cell in the local jail and whipped him until his entire body was criss-crossed with ugly red welts. In Montgomery, Ala., a homemade bomb wrecked the home of the Rev. Robert Graetz, Caucasian pastor of the Negro Trinity Lutheran Church; another bomb shattered the dwelling of the Rev. Ralph Abernathy, vice-president of the Montgomery Improvement Association; soon, five more bombs wrecked Negro churches, a Negro service station was burned to the ground and a Negro taxi driver was dragged from his car and beaten. In Camden, S. C., a patrol of hooded men seized Guy Hutchins, the director of the local high school band, and beat him—according to local accounts—"within an inch of his life."

Police did not always turn their backs on these activities. In North Carolina, local law enforcement agencies cooperated with the F.B.I. in bringing to justice at least 100 Klan night-riders. At Tabor City, ten Kluxers—who had dragged a Caucasian couple from their home and beaten them with a machine belt nailed to a pick handle—were hauled in on kidnapping charges, which, under the Federal "Lindbergh" law, provides for a maximum penalty of death. At Whiteville, 60 Klansmen were arrested in the beating of Mrs. Evergreen Flowers and the other Columbus County victims; Imperial Wizard Thomas Hamilton, self-appointed head of the Carolina Klans, was found guilty of conspiracy to assault and was sentenced to four years imprisonment; 15 of his subordinates got three-year sentences, and 49 others were fined an aggregate $18,250. Declared Superior Court Judge Clawson Williams: "The time has not come in North Carolina when a man must barricade himself in his home with the setting sun."

The time may not have come in North Carolina, but it certainly appeared to have come elsewhere. In Montgomery, Ala., six buses were fired upon and an unexploded bomb was found near the home of integrationist leader, the Rev. Martin Luther King. In Little Rock, Ark., three dynamite explosions were attributed by police to a truck driver named J. D. Sims, identified as a Klansman. And, in Springdale, Ala., a 34-year-old

Negro housepainter named Judge Aaron was seized from the porch of his girl friend's home, carried away to a deserted shack and castrated with razor blades; after the castration, his captors poured turpentine into the wound; the leader of the group of attackers was 31-year-old Joe Pritchett, Exalted Cyclops of the local K.K.K. den; asked why they had picked on Aaron, one of the Kluxers replied: "We just wanted some nigger at random."

As the wave of terror continued, responsible voices throughout the South were raised in alarm. So far, the atrocities of the moment hadn't rivaled the atrocities of the "old" Klan; but, it was not difficult to see in the present outburst a clear repetition of the pattern by which the previous two K.K.K. organizations had risen to power; in fact, *this* time, the Klan seemed to be moving toward the power of old more swiftly than either of its predecessors.

In Richmond, Va., a committee of Protestant, Catholic and Jewish religious leaders issued a joint statement warning of the clear implications of "the Klan's [new assault of] terrorist tactics and its appeals to the evil passions of hatred and bigotry." *The Richmond Times-Dispatch* echoed the warning and declared: "Virginia doesn't *want* to be saved by these horn-swogglers and fervent seekers after boodle." In Alabama, *The Gadsden Times* editorially viewed the new outbreak of K.K.K. terrorism as a combination of atrocities "which should be outlawed, vigorously opposed by decent, law-abiding citizens. What right can the K.K.K. possibly claim to flaunt itself before the Church? It does *indeed* burn the Cross." And in Tennessee, *The Chattanooga News-Free Press* a staunch *advocate* of segregation—condemned the hooded order as "a skeleton in the South's closet, a shame to be apologized for, a source of embarrassment and no benefit to the South. If the South relies upon bedsheets and burning crosses, if misguided individuals seek recourse through whip and gun, if violence becomes an accepted tool, then the South not only will lose in its efforts to maintain its traditions, but will deserve the defeat."

But, for every voice such as these, there were *other* voices—such as that of Arkansas' bellicose governor, Orval Faubus, who stated: "If it is true that the Klan is reorganizing, then it's a direct result of the improper use of Federal power." With pronouncements such as these coming from the highest elective officers of a state, it is little wonder that the Klan was able to launch a Second Comeback; indeed, in Faubus' own state, there were by the summer of 1959 no fewer than three different, overtly operating K.K.K. networks: the U. S. Klans, Knights of the Ku Klux Klan, presided over by A. C. Hightower; the Original Ku Klux Klan, headed by a transplant from Dallas, Tex., and the Association of Arkansas Klans, whose posters openly proclaimed "white supremacy" and segregation.

Alabama, too, had an "embarrassment of riches," Klan-wise. And in Florida, there were so many unconnected Klans in operation that inter-Klan feuds sometimes erupted in public. One particularly ludicrous example of K.K.K. rivalry took place at Tallahassee, where robed Kluxers distributed membership applications returnable to "Bill Hendrix, P.O. Box 708, Pinellas Park, St. Petersburg." The intended implication, it would seem was that well-known Tallahassee Klansman Hendrix—who had disbanded his Southern Knights of the K.K.K. in 1953 and retired in Pinellas County—was going back into the business. But, a few weeks after the applications with Hendrix' name on them were circulated, the Florida Ku Klux Klan at Gainesville flooded the mails with this notice: "Beware of swindlers. There are certain parties using the outlawed organization known in the past as the Knights of the K.K.K. for personal gain only. They are using a Pinellas Park address. Beware."

Another inter-Klan battle broke out in Louisiana, where the Rev. Perry E. Strickland led a revolt against Imperial Wizard Eldon Lee Edwards' U. S. Klans, Knights of the Ku Klux Klan, and formed his own Independent Knights of the Ku Klux Klan. Edwards, he suggested, was using "questionable" accounting methods in his handling of the Klans' treasury. "They just told us the Klan had a balance of $300," he complained.

In Birmingham, Ala., an inter-Klan battle became so heated that gunfire erupted and two Kluxers—J. P. Tillery and Charles C. Bridges—were wounded. Police booked four men for assault with intent to murder, among them outspoken segregationists Asa Carter and Harold McBride.

In Birmingham, police officers and the state judiciary proved fiercely determined to keep the Klan from becoming a power. When Klansmen castrated Judge Aaron, cops produced four arrests in a week—and Exalted Cyclops Joe Pritchett, leader of the castrators, was sentenced to 20 years' imprisonment, the maximum penalty. The jury which found him guilty was composed exclusively of "white" Southerners and reached its verdict in a scant 40 minutes. Alabama-born Judge Alta King, in imposing the maximum sentence, declared: "This is one of the worst things ever to come before my bench. I have found nothing in the testimony to justify less than the limit."

Police of Charlotte, N.C., proved equally determined to prevent Klan hanky-panky in their jurisdiction. When a group of robed Kluxers picketed a theater showing "Island in the Sun," a film dealing with the love affair of a Caucasian woman and a Negro man, Police Chief Frank N. Littlejohn promptly shooed them off the streets. Littlejohn also jailed five Klansmen who had plotted to bomb a Charlotte Negro elementary school in 1959. The fiery police chief—who was one of the few sworn enemies of the Carolina Klan of the 1920s—perhaps had more K.K.K. arrests to his record than any other law enforcer. "[This police department] won't tolerate cross burnings and violence," he flatly declared.

Unfortunately, there are very few Frank Littlejohns in the South. Many cops (*and* police chiefs)turned a deaf ear to all complaints about the Klan, and some were even Klan members themselves. (The city council of Camden, South Carolina, thought it wise to pass an ordinance requiring all police and municipal employees to take an oath that they were not Klan members.) When Fletcher Knebel and Clark Mollenhoff investigated the Klan in 1957 for *Look* magazine, they found that "for every Dixie official who fights the Klan, there are a *dozen* who turn their backs on Klan intimidation." They further stated that they "interviewed law officers who said they knew not a single Klansman, but, within hours, any reporter could find an admitted Klansman within the officers' jurisdiction." Moreover, some cops displayed "a tolerance" that "permits the K.K.K. to escape investigation [even] during periods of violence."

One particularly noteworthy instance of Klan violence *backfiring* took place in Robeson County, North Carolina, when the Klan decided to declare war on the Lumbee Indians. Including the "red" men in their category of "enemies," the Kluxers burned three crosses outside the Lumbee reservation. When, a few days later, Klan handbills announced a fourth cross burning to take place in a field near Maxton, the Indians decided that they had had enough. In the field that night, as 75 shotgun-toting Kluxers applied kerosene to a 12-foot cross, 350 Lumbees—carrying rifles and clubs —appeared in battle formation across the road. Shouting the war-whoops of their ancestors as they raised their rifles to their eyes, the braves advanced on the Klansmen. One Indian shot out the electric light over the Klan Klokard's podium; three of his companions shot out the tires of Klansmen's cars; another group of braves ripped apart the K.K.K. microphones and public address system. Then, their vengeance having been gained, the 350 *genuine* 100 percent Americans vanished into the night.

Unlike the Lumbees, however, the Negroes—and Negro-sympathizing Caucasians—of the South were powerless against the Klan of the Second Comeback. Violence and terror continued until, by the end of the decade, the night-riders of the "new" K.K.K. had become every bit as feared as their predecessors of the Twenties.

* * *

Keeping pace with the night-riders at all times were the Klokards, those fire-and-brimstone orators who spread the message of bias and hatred everywhere they went—and they went *everywhere*: the back room of a country store was not beneath their dignity, the spotlighted stage of a huge auditorium not beyond their confident reach. Their message was the same old song: "mongrelization of the white race" . . . "Jew-nigger-Catholic conspiracy" . . . "White Anglo-Saxon Protestant supremacy." If the lyrics were slightly different, the melody remained the same; indeed, give or take a temporal qualification, the speeches of the Second Comeback Klan were almost interchangeable with those of the Invisible Empire of the 1920s—or the Confederate Knights of the 1860s!

"We're for segregation and white supremacy and upholding the law," declared J. E. (Frog) Frazer, Grand Dragon of the Florida Ku Klux Klan—and a Kluxer since 1923. "There's plenty of ways to do things within the law and sometimes we have to straighten up the officials. Fellow sells his house to a nigger in a white neighborhood and we just spread the word. He loses his business and his friends."

An echo from Elmo C. Barnard, Imperial Wizard of the Gulf Ku Klux Klan:

"We're for free speech, free press, white supremacy, free public schools—be sure you put that white supremacy in there—just laws, the pursuit of happiness and no foreign creeds. One thing we don't like is social equality and that's what the Supreme Court declared for. It's my information that a lot of money changed hands in that deal."

Money? Where did it come from?

"The N.A.A.C.P. is backed by Jew money," says the Rev. Perry E. Strickland, Grand Dragon of Louisiana's Independent Knights of the Ku Klux Klan. The motion is seconded by Robert E. Hodges, Kligrapp of a Klavern in Columbia, S. C.; there is no doubt, he maintains, that the entire integration movement in the United States has "Jewish financial backing."

A word from Edgar Taylor, Louisiana Grand Dragon

for the U. S. Klans: "The niggers are the main thing with us now. We are not fighting Jews and Catholics except where they help the niggers."

A contradiction from the South Carolina Grand Dragon of the U. S. Klans, James H. (Bick) Bickley: "I ain't got nothing against niggers. I don't believe most of them would be causing any trouble if it wasn't for the N.A.A.C.P. and the Jews. I understand there are a lot of Communists behind this thing, trying to get us to integrate with the niggers so we'll breed down the race."

A word of agreement from the Gulf Klans' Elmo C. Barnard: "All this agitation in the South is Communist-inspired."

And a synopsis from Jacksonville Kluxer Horace Maitton:

"People in other parts of the country like to think of niggers as human beings because they have hands and feet. So do apes and gorillas have hands and feet. If a nigger has a soul, I never read about it in the Bible. The only good nigger is a dead nigger."

The record spins on—the same old warped record; but one point, perhaps obscure to the casual observer, becomes increasingly significant: These men *believe* what they are saying. During the 1860s and during the 1920s, it might have been argued that the Klan movement was a scheme to enrich a few enterprising sharpies. The same argument could not be applied to the Second Comeback Klan of the 1950s; the U. S. Klans' Grand Dragon in Alabama, Alvin Horn, makes $140 per week as a free-lance electrician—and could make more if he didn't devote so much time to the Klan; Imperial Wizard Eldon Lee Edwards of the U. S. Klans works as a paint sprayer in the Fisher Body Shop at Atlanta, Ga., for $92 a week; James H. Bickley, South Carolina Grand Dragon of the U. S. Klans, is a $62-per-week carpenter. Obviously, these men are not in the same league as the Clarkes and Evanses of old, with their $1,000,000 diamond tiaras and multimillion-dollar annual grosses; obviously, these missionaries of the Second Comeback Klan are sincere and dedicated men who *believe* what they say. And, as the decade of the Second Comeback came to a close, they persuaded more and more people to embrace their beliefs.

* * *

In retrospect, it can be seen that the Klan of the Second Comeback had gone a long way toward achieving the power of its Roaring Twenties predecessor. The "new school" masked marauders had gripped entire cities in a stranglehold of fear. The only area, really, in which the "new" had failed to match the "old" was the area of state and national politics. Or, *had* it failed?

Actually, it is impossible at the present time to assess accurately the extent of the Second Comeback Klan's political inroads. There were, to be sure, no *overt* manifestations of K.K.K. control; but, the nature of subsurface political power is such that there are no overt manifestations until long after that power has been exercised. Contemporary reporters, then, can only point to what *appear* to be *suggestions* of the existence of power.

During the 1950s there were many such suggestions on the municipal levels; but, to this author's knowledge, there were only two on higher governmental levels. One of these, not fully recognizable as such until after 1960, is dealt with in detail in the following chapter. The other is described in a clipping from *The Nation*, dated August 4, 1951:

> The Ku Klux Klan, handicapped by the "anti-mask" statutes that were recently enacted in a number of Southern states and communities, has evidently decided to mask its bigotry in the guise of politics. On June 21 the Grand Dragon of the Florida Klan, one Bill Hendrix, spoke in Jacksonville's Hemming Park not as a Dragon but as a candidate for governor. The fact that Hendrix had not qualified as a candidate—the filing date is far in the future—did not deter Mayor Hayden M. Burns from

roping off the park and nearby streets for the meeting. Significantly, the request for authorization to hold the meeting was made through a local attorney who is chairman of the Democratic Party of Duval County. A "fiery summons" sent to neighboring "klaverns" resulted in an impressive "klavalcade." Robed but unmasked Klansmen paraded through the streets protected by a permit from the mayor and a police escort. Public attention was successfully focused on the meeting by a flurry of "fiery K's" touched off a week earlier in Jacksonville, Miami and other cities. In Miami cards used to advertise the meeting carried the familiar Hitlerian thesis: "Behind every Communist is a Kike Jew." Copies of *Common Sense*, a virulently anti-Semitic sheet published in New Jersey, were also distributed. While the Klan has frequently participated in politics, this is the first time in recent years that an admitted Klan Dragon has campaigned for the governorship of a Southern state. The Klan may have been unmasked, but its postwar growth has been continuous if not spectacular; scarcely a week goes by without some Klan "bombing" or other outrage being reported in the Negro press.

Twelve years after the Jacksonville rally, the city had become a hotbed of racial tension. And, in 1964, Jacksonville Mayor Hayden M. Burns (cited in the above clipping) had defeated Miami's outspokenly integrationist Mayor Robert King High for the Democratic nomination for governor of the state of Florida. (Candidate Burns has *not*, to the best of the author's knowledge, ever publicly solicited the support of the Ku Klux Klan, nor has he ever been proved to be associated with the organization in any way; therefore it is the author's belief that any similarity between the rise of his political fortunes and the rise of Klan power in his state is purely coincidental.)

*   *   *

Before leaving the Second Comeback Klan, one final item—which is, to coin a cliché, the icing on the birthday cake. It comes from *The Birmingham (Alabama) News* of March 8, 1960.

HOUSTON, Tex.—A band of masked white youths hung a negro by his heels last night and carved two series of K.K.K.'s into his chest and stomach in reprisal for recent sit-in demonstrations by negro students at Texas Southern University.

Felton Turner, 27-year-old unemployed awning worker, told police that he was walking near his home in a negro section at 10:15 last night when a car with four masked white youths pulled up, grabbed him and forced him to come with them. They drove to a wooded area where he was tied and hung from a tree by his heels. The youths beat him with chains, cut off his clothes and carved K's about three inches high into his stomach and chest.

One of the white youths said the wounds were in reprisal for sit-ins at lunch counters in Houston by Texas Southern University negro students. A group of students from the all-negro university staged their first sit-in Friday at a lunch counter in a supermarket. The sit-in spread to a drugstore Saturday and a third store yesterday.

Police Lt. Breckenridge Porter said he is looking into the possibility that the wounds were self-inflicted.

9

THE ROBED FUHRER

"All I have to do is lift this receiver or use my car radio and I'll have a thousand men lined up in half an hour ready for the kill."
—IMPERIAL WIZARD R. N. (BOB) SHELTON,
    Tuscaloosa, Ala., 1963

ROBERT N. (BOB) SHELTON looks like a sad grasshopper. His torso is short and skeletal. His thin arms and legs are disproportionately long. When he talks, he leans forward—and you get the impression that any second he's going to bound over your head and across the room.

All in all, he's the last person in the world whom you'd expect to hold the lofty title, Imperial Wizard, United Klans of America, Knights of the Ku Klux Klan, Inc. For one thing, he doesn't look as though his nerves could take it—all he'd have to do is back into another bedsheet-bedecked Kluxer at a rally some dark night and he'd jump clear out of his skin. For another, his serious mien suggests that he is above such frivolity and pseudopomp. For still another, his soft blue eyes and his sallow face testify to a sensitivity, a *humanity,* which is totally incompatible with the means and ends of the ill famed Invisible Empire. In a sense, Shelton —ludicrous grasshopper-like bearing and all—appears to be too much of a *man* to have to be a Klansman.

All of which goes to prove that looks can be deceiving, because he's bossman of the whole damned menagerie.

It was Shelton who, when the Rev. James J. Reeb was clubbed to death by white-supremist hooligans on a Selma, Ala., street corner, shrugged off the incident because the hapless minister supposedly "had been dying of cancer before he ever came to Alabama."

It was he who, when civil rights worker Mrs. Viola Liuzzo was savagely shot to death by four Kluxers in a passing car, calmly attributed her demise to the "trumped-up plot" of "Communists and sex perverts" who wanted to "frame the Ku Klux Klan."

And it was he who, after President Lyndon B. Johnson took to national television to condemn the K.K.K. as "a society of hooded bigots," baldfacedly declared:

"He's a damn liar . . . I think he's got it reversed. He's got the shoe on the other foot."

Who *is* Shelton? Where did he come from? Where is he going? How has he managed to keep out from behind bars during the interim? What's his game? What manner of man is he?

Some men who know him describe him as "stern." Others say "dedicated." Still others say "dangerous." *Still* others say "stern, dedicated *and* dangerous." Reese Cleghorn, one of the South's most respected newsmen, has termed him one of the "five most influential men in the Southern Resistance." A Tuscaloosa Klansman offered this amendment to the description: *"One* of five, hell! Bob Shelton is *the* leader. If there's anybody in the South today who's got influence—and that includes John Patterson when he was governor here, or George Wallace now, or Ross Barnett over in Mississippi or Leander Perez in Louisiana—if *anybody's* got influence, it's Bob Shelton!"

When Shelton first appeared on the scene, his influence was limited to the service station across the street from the University of Alabama's Tuscaloosa campus, where he was a pump jockey.

Even then, however, he was a man to be reckoned

with. In 1958, State Attorney General John C. Patterson polled a nearly incredible 34,000-vote plurality in the Democratic gubernatorial primaries against a field of 14 rabid segregationists, including Circuit Judge George C. Wallace. Most observers feel that this smashing victory was at least partly the result of Patterson's having obtained the mailing list of the K.K.K. monthly hate sheet, *The Fiery Cross,* and having pitched the Kluxers—on his official Attorney General stationery—in the name of "a mutual friend, Mr. R. N. (Bob) Shelton."

Shelton and his Kluxers campaigned actively for Patterson's election. After the victory, Shelton boasted publicly that Patterson was a winner only because of K.K.K. support. Patterson never admitted to Klan influence on his administration (who would?), but he never publicly denied Shelton's boast—and he never repudiated Klan support.

Shortly after Patterson took office, the Alabama legislature undertook consideration of a proposition to expand the state's mental hospital facilities. Shelton opposed the proposition with this statement: "I am against giving any more money to the insane hospitals or to the University of Alabama Medical College, which is the rottenest place in Alabama. I am not opposed to helping the Alabama folks who are mentally ill, but I want the program to be completely separate from the National Mental Health Association, which has been linked with the Communists. As long as they have those alien psychiatrists at the mental hospitals and at the University Medical College, as long as they have those doctors who talk broken English with an alien accent, then I do not favor giving them any more money at all."

After Shelton's speech, Governor Patterson announced his opposition to the plan. It died on the assembly floor.

The big rift between Shelton and Patterson came in 1959, when Patterson endorsed Senator John F. Kennedy's bid for the Democratic presidential nomination. A few days after the announcement of Patterson's endorsement, the governor was visited by a 32-man delegation commanded by the Imperial Kladd of the Prattville, Ala., Klavern and was asked:

"Did it ever occur to you that you are being used as a guinea pig by the Communist-Jewish integrators to sample the political sentiment of the South for John Kennedy?"

Also: "How much money will the Jewish firms of the arch-integrationist and avowed enemy of the South, [ex-New York Senator] Herbert Lehman make out of the $20 million [in road bonds bought by his family's firm, Lehman Brothers] you arranged for Lehman Brothers to undertake?"

In the subsequent gubernatorial elections, Shelton and his Kluxers backed Wallace—who won handily each time. Patterson went the way of all losers . . .

* * *

In his office at Suite 401 of the Alston Building in Tuscaloosa, R. N. (Bob) Shelton—consort of governors and leader of Klansmen—sat back and massaged his perpetually furrowed forehead with long, bony fingers.

The wave of Klan violence had not yet begun, and in the calm before the storm, the Imperial Wizard outlined his plans for what could only be called the Klan of the Buttoned-Down Bedsheet.

"We are projecting a new image of the Klan," he told an interviewer. "People keep accusing the Klan of wrongdoing and forgetting all the good things we're doing—like, we give people food for Christmas, help needy children, pay up rent for a poor fellow or help a man if his house burns down. We're launching a new campaign called 'Ballots, Not Bullets.'

"You might ask the question: Why, if you wanted to have [such] an organization, why not pick another name besides the Ku Klux Klan? The Ku Klux Klan was the only organization that was organized, formulated and put into effect by Americans, inside American shorelines. So why should you throw away a heritage and a principle. My grandfather was a member.

My father was a member. Because you have people who are associated through their families with the Klan association, many people are sympathetic with the Klan whether they are in it or not."

But what, it was asked, of the Klan's long and widespread reputation as a terrorist, hate-mongering and murderous organization?

"We are a law-abiding organization, observing the duly constituted authority of the law—and we are not going out provoking or asking trouble or trying to bring about violence. But we are certainly going to maintain self-preservation. The law of nature calls for self-preservation. I'm not going out looking for trouble, or violence, but if it comes to us, we're going to protect ourselves."

Exactly what sort of violence did Shelton feel might come to him?

His greatest fear, he declared, was of a "nigger uprising"—which, from where he sat, was both inevitable and imminent.

"It's in the planning stage [now]," he explained. "It's not going to be too long, from activities coming out of Cuba being withheld from the general public. I can see, from conditions that exist today, the upsurging of the nigger element through guidance of the Communist conspiracy. And I don't mean Northerner against Southerner—this is definitely going to lead to a violent revolution between the black man and the white man. There will be no straddling of the fence. And definite evidence has already been shown—actions in Leopoldville, in the Congo—what will happen when you give these niggers, these crazed savages, the power. So it is something that there will have to be a solution to—a drastic solution, immediately."

Did he have any specific drastic solution in mind?

"F. D. R. gave us some of it. We have the fleet in mothballs that could be brought out for transportation back to Africa, and we have the storage of food in Alaska that runs into the billions and billions, which gives them the food. And we also have in Africa over $11 billion worth of storage homes that belong to the federal government. The only thing that Roosevelt didn't supply was a leader, and I think that the niggers could select their own leader who could send them back as colonies to Africa. Let them have their own government. Let them advance their own strategy and have their social equality."

Did he believe then, like Imperial Wizard Hiram Wesley Evans in the 1920s, that the Negro was incapable of "assimilating" into Anglo-Saxon society?

"Absolutely!" he snapped. "The nigger is a diseased animal and can never be our equal. If he was forced into captivity in coming to America, what's so bad about forcing him into captivity and carrying him back to his home?"

Then, did he believe that it was totally impossible to achieve an integrated society—or, at least, to maintain the status quo?

"If things are left as they are," he said, "there's no question but that we will have a revolution of the black man against the white man; unless some drastic steps are taken by conservative-thinking people to head off this Communist trend of using niggers as tools, aggravating them into these dastardly acts. We are all the time reading in the medias that this is a nonviolent demonstration, but there has never been any demonstration carried out by them that has not had violence connected. They have that savage instinct."

Was the immediate aim of the Klan, then, to bring about Federal legislation that would ship all Negroes back to Africa?

"Our aim," said the Imperial Wizard, "is to educate our own people to the conspiracy between Jews, niggers and Communists to take over our government. Uneducated people are useless, so our main objective is education. I go around and speak before various Klans and civic groups, like the P. T. A. I tell them I'm from the Ku Klux Klan and I want to speak with you on the Nigger-Jewish-Communist conspiracy."

The repeated reference to a "Communist conspiracy," finally coupled with the mention of fluoridation, automatically invokes in the mind of anyone who has seen the satiric motion picture *Dr. Strangelove: Or How I Learned to Stop Worrying and Love the Bomb,* the image of General Jack D. Ripper setting loose a wing of hydrogen-bomb-carrying B-52s on Russia—because he feared a Communist conspiracy to poison the "natural bodily fluids" of America through fluoridation.

Did the city of Tuscaloosa have a fluoridation program? Shelton was asked. And was he opposed to it?

"Yes, damn it," he replied, "flouridation has been here five years. They slipped it in here without people voting on it or even knowing about it until recently. It's a Communist plot. What's a better way to take over this country than to give an overdose of fluoridation? It would go to people's brains and paralyze them so they wouldn't care about anything. They wouldn't even know!"

General Jack D. Ripper, *Strangelove* fans will remember, was a God-fearing man. Was Shelton also? He was.

"I'm a Methodist," he said. "I have a wife and three kids. They're all Methodists."

Did he go along with the teachings of his church?

"I fall out with 90 percent of most of them. They teach alien ideologies like the Judeo-Christian heritage. They talk about whiskey and hurting people's feelings. But race—here's where I fall out with them—race is more important than whiskey. They've been brainwashed by the Jews in the National Council of Churches. They don't even want to *talk* about the race issue."

Did he think, then, that the Jews should be feared as much as the possiblity of a Negro revolt?

"We all know that the nigger ain't smart enough to manipulate the moves he's making. It's the Jews who are in back of this. Did the N-Double-A-C-P ever have a nigger president? No! I don't hate niggers, but I hate the Jews. The nigger's a child, but the Jews are dangerous people. All their pseudo-intellectuals from Harvard and their low moral standards. All they want is control and domination of the Gentiles through a conspiracy with the niggers."

The interjection of his concept of Jewish "moral standards" automatically brings to mind the sexual paranoia of Thomas E. Watson. Did Imperial Wizard Shelton share his predecessor's erotic fears?

"My grandfather died for the virtues of the white man," said Shelton. "He died for me, and if I don't stand up for what he stood up for, I ain't much of a man. Unborn generations will suffer. Already, sex morals have been trampled down in the North. Why, niggers account for more than 75 percent of the venereal diseases in this country. Did you know that there's a rape in this country every thirty-four-and-a-half minutes?"

He was also concerned about *voluntary* sexual relations between Negroes and Caucasians—whether legalized by marriage or not; such liaisons could only result in the "breeding down of the white race."

"Any nation that ever failed in history," he said, "failed because of the amalgamation of the races. The Bible itself teaches segregation all the way through it. In ancient Egypt, in Rome, in Greece, they all failed because the niggers came and mingled and destroyed their great civilizations."

Did Shelton then think that the Negro is *generically* inferior to the Caucasian?

"I think history has proven that. The white race of people have had a cultured civilization for over 2,000 years. The nigger has only been out of the savage actions of the jungles of Africa for approximately 200 years. And the niggers had the same opportunity and resources in Africa to develop himself and his race of people as our forefathers had in America. I think we can all realize that the nigger does not have the initiative, the basic intelligence, to be creative—does not have the ingenuity to devise, invent, create things that the white race does."

* * *

It is easy, of course, to rebut Shelton's contentions. The argument of generic inferiority defeats itself; the notion of an international Jew-Negro-Communist conspiracy leaves itself open not merely to *reductio ad absurdum,* but to *reductio ad hilaritatem*. Yet, it must be remembered that Shelton does not bring these arguments and notions before an impartial panel of rhetorical experts; he brings them, *unchallenged,* to an audience of men and women who from the cradle have been conditioned to accept them as gospel. Indeed, Shelton *himself* has from the cradle been prepared to dedicate his life to their promulgation — and he does promulgate them, not because he is an evil man, or even a sick one, but because he is a *sincere* man who is tragically misinformed.

One thinks again of *Dr. Strangelove's* Jack D. Ripper and the consequences of his acting upon his erroneous beliefs. The parallel with Shelton is frightening. Ripper, fortunately, is fiction; Shelton is fact.

10

THE SIEGE OF ST. AUGUSTINE

"The stage is being set for the earth to get a bloodbath. When the smoke clears, there ain't going to be nothing left except white faces."

THE REV. CHARLES CONLEY LYNCH,
St. Augustine, Fla., 1963

AS WORD CAME from Washington, D.C., that the House of Representatives had taken under consideration what would soon become the Civil Rights Act of 1964, members of the Ku Klux Klan began to formulate plans for a mass resistance movement. No single Klan headquarters or Klavern could be identified as the nucleus of this movement; but, with each individual within each suborganization working in his own way toward the same goal—prevention of the Negro's assuming his God-given and Constitutionally reaffirmed rights as a human being—the groundwork was laid for the greatest display of mass lawlessness since the days of the Confederacy.

Ironically, the state in which this odious rebellion came to a head was Florida—the one Southern state generally considered to be most "liberal" on the civil rights question. It is now apparent that this was less a case of accident than of design.

Throughout 1931, the Klan had been stoking the Floridian fires of insurrection with Hitlerian fervor. K.K.K. Klokards had conducted rallies, cross burnings and parades in every part of the state. Hate literature had been distributed by the ream. Even "outside" mercenaries—notably the allegedly Reverend Charles Conley Lynch, of California—had been imported to rouse the rabble in areas where inept local yokels could not do the job.

In St. Petersburg, an organization calling itself The Church of Jesus Christ, Christian founded in 1946 by a former Ku Klux Klan rifle-team instructor named Wesley Swift, announced the formation of "guerilla warfare units . . . designed to defend the country in case of a take-over [presumably, by Negroes]." The Rev. Oren Potito, St. Petersburg-based president of the organization's Eastern Conference, declared: "We have regular rifle practice, and our members go on maneuvers with jeeps and boats . . . " An organization of apparently similar scope—though without claims of a "church" connection or divine "mission"—was St. Augustine's Ancient City Hunting Club, headed by one "Hoss" Muncey. (It was Muncey, incidentally, who led an assault on Negroes attempting to swim at St. Augustine's "whites-only" beach in 1964.) Further documentation of sub-Klan armed terrorism is provided by Hearst columnist Victor Riesel, who discovered individual

"Wolfpacks" whose "females carry revolvers in their handbags" and whose "menfolk practice shooting, grenade throwing (using rocks), torture techniques and terror bombing on river banks and ocean fronts." Riesel adds: "They have a swift courier service to avoid using the easily-tapped telephones. They can raise 100-car caravans in half an hour."

None of these activities was conducted in total secrecy. In fact, responsible voices throughout the state repeatedly called public attention to the dangers which lay ahead. The Florida Region, National Conference of Christians and Jews, distributed documented reports of hate groups' movements toward strength; the Florida Council on Human Relations infiltrated Klan meetings and made available detailed accounts of what transpired; Bill Baggs, editor of *The Miami News,* published front-page editorials urging steps to prevent the outbreak of racial violence.

In September of 1963, handbills were distributed throughout St. Augustine inviting "all white people" to attend a rally of the Ku Klux Klan. The site of the get-together was a clearing at the edge of the woods approximately half a mile off U. S. Highway #1—outside of the city limits. Among those in attendance at the rally (most assuredly *not* as a Klansman) was Irving Cheney, associate director of the Florida Council on Human Relations. It is to him that we are indebted for this comprehensive—and chilling—report:

> "On turning off the highway, I noticed a number of robed and hooded men, most of whom were directing the parking of cars. No law enforcement officer was in evidence, either at the highway for directing traffic or at the meeting to insure orderly procedure. A dozen or more children, ranging in age from eight to twelve, were positioned at irregular intervals along the lane. They were selling Confederate automobile tags.
>
> "I was told by a hooded man that I might drive all the way to the end of the road or park alongside the road. I chose to park halfway between the highway and the meeting place, backing into my

parking place in case a hasty exit were indicated.

"No sooner had I arrived at the clearing than a red-robed Klansman ordered the lighting of the cross. It was my first experience at seeing this well-known desecration of the time-honored Christian symbol, and I felt a sense of revulsion at it. A huge cross, possibly 20 feet high, had been wrapped in burlap, soaked in flammable liquid and placed in an upright position. A match was applied and the cross was immediately covered with flames. Robed Klansmen and Klanswomen, two dozen strong, walked in a circle around the burning cross, giving a sort of sloppy, left-handed sign of obeisance. It was vaguely reminiscent of the *sieg-heil* salute of the Nazi's.

"As this procession occurred, one could hear the faint strains of *The Old Rugged Cross* floating across the crowd. A group of girls, early teen-agers, were humming and singing as the fire became more and more intense . . .

"It was mildly amusing to note that this extreme racist group was robed in three colors—white, red and black. It seemed ironical that white and black should be mixed so freely in such a meeting, though one sensed that the black was coldly symbolic."

As Cheney watched, the meeting was called to order by one of the hooded terrorists. "Our Brother Klansman Gene F." was summoned to "lead in the invocation."

"Oh, God," intoned Gene F., "we thank You for this occasion which brings these good white people together. We know that it is Your good will that we be here, that we be stirred to the fact that we've got to fight for what You've given us. All we want is to do Your precious will. Help us to be ready to fight, to shed blood if necessary, to maintain our way of life. In Jesus' precious name we pray, Amen."

The presiding officer then returned to the podium to introduce "our speaker of the evening . . . a man who has been a minister of the gospel for more than 35 years. It is my pleasure to introduce to you Brother Connie Lynch, of Alabama."

"Brother" Lynch "of Alabama" is the Rev. Charles Conley Lynch, a 51-year-old native of Clarksville, Tex. He is, by profession, *literally* a merchant of hate. Unencumbered by a formal education (he quit school after the ninth grade), he was ordained in 1936 as a minister in the General Assembly of Jesus Christ, a 20-year-old sect in California. "I never attended no seminaries," he admitted once; "I just got my credentials."

During World War II, he was drafted and assigned to a basic training unit at Camp Barkeley, Tex. After additional training at Camp Butner, N. C., he was reassigned to the Sixth Replacement Depot as a cook. His Klan followers in recent years have referred to him as a "war hero" and a "Jap-killer;" but, if he single-handedly wiped out any enemy battalions, it was by voodoo—because the U. S. Army has no record of it. (He *did,* however, incur an injury on the Pacific Island of New Caledonia in 1943—when a gas stove in his kitchen exploded.)

After the war with Japan was over, Lynch returned to the United States to declare war against the Negro —or, in his term, to prevent "the eventual distruction of the white race" by "mongrelization." He allied himself with the Western Conference of The Church of Jesus Christ, Christian—the organization previously cited as having been founded by a one-time K.K.K. rifle-team instructor—and proceeded to sew the seeds of racial hatred all over the state of California.

In the mid-1950s, he became a free-lance preacher, travelling all over the United States to warn of the "evil conspiracy of race mixing." In his travels, he accused presidents Roosevelt, Truman, Eisenhower (and later, Kennedy and Johnson) of having "played a part in the sell-out of this country" to an alleged international Jewish conspiracy, which he claimed he could prove responsible for the Revolutionary War, the Civil War, World War I, World War II, and the Korean conflict. (Presumably, the War of 1812 and the Spanish-American War were non-Semitically caused.)

In 1962, he went to work as an organizer in California for the National States Rights Party—an organization termed by the House Un-American Activities Committee as "more potentially dangerous than any of the American Nazi groups, as it is interested in activities that are far more vigorous and direct . . ." He was subsequently *bounced* by that group because he was found to be too militant, even for *them*. In explaining Lynch's dismissal, the information director of the National States Rights Party, Dr. Edward Fields, said: "He was too extreme . . . He organized his group with black belts, boots and helmets!"

In March of 1963, Lynch and two associates were found guilty of battery and disturbing the peace in San Bernardino, Calif.; they had attacked a group of teen-agers in a restaurant parking lot and wounded one with five pellets from a gas-propelled gun; but they were released after paying a fine of $1,200. Lynch has also been arrested in Gadsden, Ala., and held for questioning by police in Little Rock, Ark., and Memphis, Tenn. "I'm no stranger to a jail," he boasted once; "I can sleep there as good as any hotel."

In 1963, he was brought into St. Augustine—according to one report, by attorney J. B. Stoner, former Imperial Wizard of the Christian Knights of the Ku Klux Klan. *Life* magazine identified Stoner as "an extremist who is under heavy F.B.I. surveillance" and said that he "came down from Georgia" to organize "a rough and tough Klan, looking for action."

Taking the podium at the K.K.K. rally where the Florida Council on Human Relations' Associate Director Irvin Cheney was present, Lynch spoke—according to Cheney—as follows:

> "My friends, I want to share with you something of the history, the glorious history, of the Klan. The Klan was born out of bloodshed, out of a real need to protect the Southern white man from the carpet-baggers—the Jew carpet-baggers. You know,

of course, that the carpet-baggers was Jews, and they come down here and teamed up with the niggers and tried to take away everything that the white man had. But they learned that the white man would not take all this lying down. He organized. He organized into Klans. He 'rose up to defend his honor and his interests. And, I'll tell you that to this day, the Jews, the niggers and all the rest of the colored people are not afraid of anything else—but they are afraid of the Klan.

"For the last 30 years, the Klan has not been strong, has not been militant. But the Klan is on the move again, and it is not going to let the niggers and the Jews take over our country.

"Now, some of you say: 'But, Jesus was a Jew.' That just goes to show you how these cotton-pickin', half-witted preachers had fooled you. Jesus wasn't no Jew, he was a white man. Jesus said that the Jews was descended from Cain, the cursed side of creation. He said that they was children of the devil. So don't let no sentimental fool tell you that Jesus was a Jew.

"I've been through a lot of battles in my time, and I am still battling for what I know is right. I'm speaking for God, and you'd better hear what I say.

"Not long ago, a man from the F.B.I.—you know what that is, the Federal Bureau of Integration—come by to talk to me. I'll guarantee you there's some of them here in this crowd tonight and some of them Jew bastards from the Anti-Defamation League of B'nai B'rith is here, too. They always spy on me.

"But anyhow, they come by and said, 'Now you don't really advocate violence, do you?'

"And I said, 'The hell you say. The niggers has declared all-out war on the plan of God, and on God's family, the white man—and, in war, you shoot!'

"Then they said to me, 'Do you know who bombed the church in Birmingham?'

"And I said, 'No, and if I did, I wouldn't tell you.'

"But I'll tell you people here tonight, if they can find these fellows, they ought to pin medals on them. Someone said, 'Ain't it a shame that them little children was killed?'

"Well, they don't know what they are talking about. In the first place, they ain't little. They're 14 or 15 years old—old enough to have venereal diseases, and I'll be surprised if all of 'em didn't have one or more.

"In the second place, they weren't children. Children are little *people*, little *human beings*, (Italics, Cheney's.) and that means white people.

"There's little dogs and cats and apes and baboons and skunks and there's also little niggers. But they ain't children. They're just little niggers.

"And, in the third place, it wasn't no shame they was killed. Why? Because, when I go out to kill rattlesnakes, I don't make no difference between little rattlesnakes and big rattlesnakes, because I know it is the nature of all rattlesnakes to be my enemies and to poison me if they can. So I kill 'em all, and if there's four less niggers tonight, then, I say, 'Good for whoever planted the bomb.' We're all better off.

"Some people say that we'll all be in heaven together. The hell we will! Only God's family will be in heaven, and niggers and Jews ain't in God's family. Ain't gonna be no animals in heaven, and ain't gonna be no sons of perdition there.

"It's just a shame some people brought these black animals over here, animals highly enough developed so that their seed can mix with your seed.

"But they won't be here much longer, because the Klan is getting stronger. People up North are begging us to come up there to help them organize. Imagine that! They've decided they don't like the niggers too well, either, and they want help. And we are busy and growing in the South.

"I believe in violence, all the violence it takes either to scare the niggers out of the country or to have 'em all six feet under. My old daddy told me never to trust that old kicking mule we had, and never to trust a nigger. That was good advice.

"Some of the niggers say, 'We want to go to your churches.' There ain't but one manly thing— Christian thing—to do when they try, and that is to meet 'em at the church house door with a base-ball bat and to beat their brains out.

"I'll tell you something else. You've got a nigger in St. Augustine ought not to live . . . that burr-headed bastard of a dentist. He's got no right to live at all, let alone walk up and down your streets and breathe the white man's free air.

"He ought to wake up tomorrow morning with a bullet between his eyes. If you were half the men you claim to be, you'd kill him before sunup."

At this point, Cheney relates, an elderly bystander shouted, "Tell us about King!"

Lynch replied:

"Oh, you mean Martin Luther Coon! That's the biggest enemy we've ever had. He's crooked as a snake. He ought to have been killed a long time ago. I heard him on TV the other night saying, 'The NEEEgro is not satisfied.' (The Southern pronunciation of Negro is "nigra"—hence Lynch's stress.) Well, he never will be, because before they are satisfied they all will be six feet under the ground.

"That Elijah Muhammed (head of the militantly antiwhite Black Muslim sect) said the other day that they were ready to sacrifice 10 million niggers in their fight.

"Well now, that's just fine—because if they are willing to sacrifice 10 million, I'll be more than happy to help them sacrifice the other 10 million!

"They want to mix with you, do they? Well, listen: if you mix ice cream and axle grease, you don't hurt the axle grease much at all—but you play hell with the ice cream.

"In spite of what those numb-skull idiots on the Supreme Court say, they ain't got no right to mix with you and don't you let 'em.

"If you have to fight and shed blood, theirs or yours, do it!

"You won't hear the white man whining when he has a few casualties like the niggers do. They scream and cry about those dead animals in Birmingham. The niggers started the war, and when you start a war, you expect some to die. More will die, and you'd better be ready to see to it that they do.

"I'm speaking for God, and you'd better listen.

"We've got guts enough to do something about the situation and no other organization has. We need a good strong group in St. Augustine. You come and sign up. But don't come if you are weak or a coward. This ain't no peaceful organization. We aim to do whatever is necessary to put the nigger back in his place—preferably in his grave."

* * *

As Trevor Armbister observed in *The Saturday Evening Post,* "the menace of Connie Lynch and of the scores of others like him lies not in what they say, for countless persons are uttering similar diatribes with no appreciable effect. Lynch's talent is in knowing where to say it, and how."

The truth of the observation has never been more apparent than at the St. Augustine rally. Lynch's speech, Cheney relates, lasted one hour and fifteen minutes; it was met with "frenzied, screaming approval and rebel yells"; the crowd was emotionally "at fever pitch."

Shortly after the speech was over, there came shouts from the bushes near the speakers' platform.

"Niggers! Niggers! Niggers!"

Apparently, some Negroes had infiltrated the Konklave and were hiding out in the shrubbery.

Cheney's report continues:

"Frantically, Connie Lynch jumped from the platform and jerked a gun from his coral-colored Cadillac, cocking it as he handed it to another man. Another gun appeared as if from out of the air and large knives, sticks and brass knuckles appeared on all sides.

"Twenty or more men went into the bushes to the north and in a few moments, they brought four Negro men to the platform. Each Negro was prodded by a knife or a gun in his back. There were all sorts of taunts, vile, vicious, frantic.

" 'Boy, what're y'all doing out here?'

" 'We just came out to run our fish lines,' came the reply . . .

"Two young men, whom I observed closely, held guns toward their captives, while no one seemed to know what to do. There was considerable swaggering and big talk, but a look at the faces of those who held the weapons indicated that they were perplexed and afraid. A few moments before it had been easy for them to scream approval of 'killing all the niggers,' but now holding real weapons and faced with real people, they hardly knew what to do . . .

"[But] if the white men had fears and were reluctant to do harm, their women took care of that. They cajoled, shouted and prodded the men into action. Children joined in the chorus of demands that the Negroes be killed.

"At this point, two white men stripped their (the Negroes') shirts away and began to strike with their fists. At the sight of blood, I finally was jolted into an awareness of the fact that this was, indeed, a tragically real occurrence . . .

"Having observed the confusion and cowardice written in the men's faces, I had a fleeting impulse to step forward and to say: 'All right, I am a white Southerner, too, but you've lost your minds. Shoot these men if you wish, but shoot through me. Come on, fellows, let's go,' and then take them (the Negroes) to my car.

"I still wonder if calling their bluff in this way

might not have worked. I must say, however, any plan to follow such a course was short-lived.

"The beating continued, the women persisting with:

" *'Castrate the bastards!'*

" *'Kick their balls out!'*

" *'Knock their heads off!'*

" *'Kill 'em. Come on, do something! They had to trespass to get here, they've got no right to live. String 'em up.'*

"Nearby, a robed woman spoke in a semi-whisper to her husband:

" *'Go get the head chopper . . . and get the rope, and for God's sake, take off your robe and leave it in the car. You don't want to mess it up.'*

"It was then I knew I had to leave the crowd, make my way to a telephone and summon police help. But I was almost in the middle of the mob, and to get away was extremely precarious. My automobile was a quarter mile away. The people had been reminded repeatedly that 'spies' doubtless were present. No one else was leaving at this time, and there was no certainty that a person leaving would not be shot.

"At each blow of the fist and responding shout from the crowd, I managed to take a few steps through the mob, and to take up a new position for a few seconds. Finally, after an eternity of seconds, I had worked my way to the extreme edge of the gathering. There then was nothing to do but to saunter casually toward my automobile, kicking aimlessly in the sand as I walked along. Once in my car, I left quickly but not at excessive speed . . .

"[After finding a public telephone], I called the sheriff's office and reported the incident. The way in which I was answered with, 'Is that so? Thank you,' left me with the feeling that he almost had been expecting such a call . . . Aware that local law enforcement had been reputed to be somewhat inequitable along racial lines, I still feared that nothing might be done in time to save the four

Negroes. I had known that Negroes recently had been arrested and sentenced for 'littering' when they passed out handbills. I knew also that the Ku Kluxers had not been arrested for doing the same thing on that day, or rather that some had been brought in and released, the police saying, 'but they weren't littering.'

"Having this anxiety, my next step was to call the state Adjutant General's office. I was required to give considerable information about myself before making a report on the current fracas, but someone in that office did take the information from me.

"Still wondering if enough had been done, I then placed a long distance call to the F.B.I. in Jacksonville . . . It seemed to me that both federal and local laws were being flaunted and that each agency at least should have the information, beginning on the local level and going to the top . . .

"I then drove back to a bowling alley which was by the entrance to the wood road [where the Klan *Konklave* was being held] and parked in front of it. A small group of young men from the rally had gathered by the corner of the bowling alley [suggesting that the rally was over] . . . After about 10 minutes, I saw a green unmarked automobile pass, in which were two officers and the four Negroes. With this, I felt free to leave and I headed for home.

"Since then, I have learned that four white men from among the mob were arrested on a charge of assault and battery, and that they were released on $100 bond each. This, incidentally, is as small as the smallest bond exacted of the Negroes in recent demonstrations. Some have been as high as $750.

"The sheriff is reported to have said that by the time of his arrival, the crowd had dwindled down to nothing. However, as I left the bowling alley to return home, I looked down the lane and there were many more than four cars still parked along the way to the meeting place. Perhaps some of these brave Klansmen and their vocal Klanswomen had made for the bushes, and perhaps only four people were still in evidence, but I have no doubt that a minimum of effort would have revealed others.

"I also learned that, while I was telephoning, the beatings became more brutal than any which I had witnessed and that three of the Negroes are hospitalized at this writing.

"To give proper credit to the sheriff, I must say that he arrived on the scene within a very few minutes after he was called."

The sheriff of St. Johns County, Florida, was L. O. Davis—described by George McMillan in *Life* as "a self-pronounced passionate believer in segregation." McMillan further revealed that "many of the several hundred local white men" deputized by the sheriff "to cope with impending racial violence" are "known to be Klan members." Sheriff Davis, McMillan stated, "has been seen at Klan meetings himself, though whether in his capacity as a law officer or as a private citizen is not clear."

*   *   *

During autumn of 1963, the Florida Advisory Committee to the U. S. Civil Rights Commission had termed St. Augustine a "segregated super-bomb" with a "short fuse." It had warned of the dangers of increased activity by Ku Klux Klan groups throughout St. Johns County. It had called attention to many Negro complaints of police brutality. It had urgently recommended that action be taken to eliminate racial discrimination in employment and public accommodations. But the commission's report fell on deaf ears.

In May of 1964, the Rev. Martin Luther King and members of the National Association for the Advancement of Colored People staged wade-ins at St. Augustine's public beach. They were followed into the water by Caucasians, who beat them with clubs, sticks and fists. Later, demonstrators dived into the swimming pool at a segregated motel. The owner of the motel ordered them out; when they refused to leave, he poured acid into the water. The owner was not jailed; the Rev. Martin Luther King was arrested—twice.

In ensuing days, organized squads of Caucasian resistance forces plowed into the ranks of Negro demonstrators and beat them unmercifully. Among the attackers were men known to be members of the Ancient City Hunting Club and/or the Ku Klux Klan. The men who were supposed to be keeping the peace—Sheriff L. O. Davis and his deputies—did not prevent the attacks. Finally, Governor Farris Bryant sent in state troopers to halt the bloodshed.

Later, Sheriff Davis was called before Federal Judge Bryan Simpson at Jacksonville and asked if he had recruited Klansmen as deputies. He replied that he had not. He was also asked if he knew what the Ancient City Hunting Club was. He replied that he did not. The judge made light of his denials and reprimanded him:

"I think, sheriff, as a law enforcement officer you can appreciate the danger in a situation like this when you have members of the Klan and allied organizations in your organization as deputies."

In June of 1964, as both Republican and Democrat leaders of the U. S. Senate struggled to bring about passage of the Civil Rights Act over a Southern filibuster, Negro demonstrators prepared to resume their nonviolent protests against discriminatory practices in St. Augustine. Activities in "Providence No. 41," the area Klavern of the Ku Klux Klan, were stepped up. The moment of truth was approaching.

There can be no doubt that the city had received ample warning of the imminent danger; but, as Trevor Armbrister pointed out in *The Saturday Evening Post,* the warnings went unheeded until even "voices of moderation grew faint. The clergy—with few exceptions—remained silent. *The St. Augustine Record* filled its pages with pictures of beauty queens. Businessmen who make up the city's 'power structure' ignored the coming conflict."

On June 24, 1964, the Rev. Charles Conley Lynch—

who had spent the spring spreading his poison in Jacksonville and elsewhere—returned to the city. With full protection from Sheriff Davis and his corps of deputies, he mounted a bench in the city's main square and proceeded to rouse the rabble.

"Martin Lucifer Coon!" he declared. "That nigger says its gonna be a hot summer. If he thinks the niggers can make it a hot summer, I will tell him that 140 million white people know how to make it a hotter summer! This great, sleeping white giant is waking up. They ask me, do you believe in violence? If it takes violence to defend our Constitution, the answer is yes!"

In later speeches, he repeated the contention of United Klans Imperial Wizard Robert Shelton that America's 20 million Negroes should be shipped back to Africa—forceably, if necessary. "I wouldn't blink an eye if it meant every nigger getting killed," he declared. He again proclaimed his "love" for the Constitution and delivered a particularly venomous harangue against "this bunch of gangsters in Washington (which) has violated it, has committed every act, from the top level of treason right on down, against the white people, against God, against this nation." Also contributing to the din was the aforementioned Attorney, J. B. Stoner, with diatribes against "that Martin Luther Coon" and "the Jew-stacked, Communist-lovin' Supreme Court." On the subject of Communism, Lynch added: "Our enemy is not Russia; it is the infiltration of this seeping cancer of Communism, this silly ideology of race mixing and brotherhood."

The riots on June 25 were, in the words of one observer, "the city's worst violence in a year"—and, in the words of another observer, "the worst racial riots in the city's 400-year history." During the night, while Negroes regrouped their forces for the next day's "nonviolent" (on their part) demonstrations, Lynch called another rally at the city's main square and declared: "I favor violence to preserve the white race . . . Now, I grant you, some niggers are going to get killed in the process, but when war's on, that's what happens."

The days that followed were carbon copies of the first.

Injured Negroes numbered well into the hundreds. The streets of St. Augustine were, quite literally, stained with blood. Later, in *Life* magazine, George McMillan offered this significant—and terrifying—analysis:

"When the civil rights demonstrations began again in earnest several weeks ago, there was simply no reasonable hope that the marchers would be protected—and everyone in St. Augustine knew it. On one hand was the mob—tough, shot through with Klan members and very well organized. It was not surprising that so many showed up. I had been told that a system of chain telephone calls allows 'most of the Klan in northern Florida to be alerted in 30 minutes.' And around the plaza I saw white men on the fringes of the action using citizens' band radios to keep track of the demonstrators' line of march and who was in the parade.

"Between the mob and its target—the marchers—stood only Sheriff Davis. The bloody results of the first clashes could have surprised no one. The demonstrators —dedicated to the principles of non-violence—were set upon by the waiting whites. They were slugged and stomped, arose to be attacked and fall again, while the sheriff's men stood by and watched. In the end a heavy force of state troopers moved in and stopped the violence."

After the demonstrations ceased, Martin Luther King left the city, but the Rev. Charles Conley Lynch remained. Telling reporters that he was "inspired, really thrilled" by the manner in which segregationist St. Augustinians had greeted him, he promised further resistance to the civil rights movement with these appalling words:

"There's going to be a bloody race riot all over this nation. The stage is being set for the earth to get a bloodbath. When the smoke clears, there ain't going to be nothing left except white faces."

11

KILL ME A NIGGER

"You'll never be able to convict a white man that kills a nigger what encroaches on the white race of the South."

WIZARD JAMES VENABLE,
Atlanta, Ga., 1964

DANIELSVILLE, GA., is a small, sleepy-looking community with a population of 362. A favorite local joke "explains" that this population always remains the same —because every time a girl has a baby, another man leaves town. Most natives react to this bawdy bit of "cracker" humor with guffaws and thigh-slapping belly-laughs. They are a serious, hard-working people, but they are not adverse to a good chuckle now and then, even if it happens to be at their own expense.

The houses lining the tree-shaded streets of Danielsville are neat and well-kept. At night, when the pleasant scent of jasmine fills the air, men and women gather in little clusters along the "main drag" and chat amiably before going home to bed. The atmosphere is a bright and cheerful one—hardly the sort of atmosphere in which one might expect a brutal and senseless racial murder to be committed. But, on the quiet and jasmine-scented morning of July 11, 1964, along a desolate country road in Madison County—of which Danielsville is the seat—such a murder took place; a murder so base and heinous that it could only be termed a wanton assassination.

The victim was Lemuel A. Penn, Director of Adult and Vocational Education for the public school system of Washington, D.C. He was slain, according to Solicitor-General Clete Johnson, only because he "came into this world with a black skin."

Penn, a Lieutenant Colonel in the U. S. Army Reserve, had left Washington in June of 1964 to attend summer training at the Infantry School, Fort Benning, Ga. On July 11, after completing classes he returned home by car. With him were two other reservists, Charles E. Brown and John D. Howard, both Negro school teachers from the Capitol.

At approximately 3:50 a.m., the group stopped at Athens, Ga., to switch drivers. Howard climbed into the back seat and fell asleep. Brown slept in the front seat and Penn took the wheel. Some 10 miles later, they entered a foggy stretch of highway near the village of Colbert in Madison County, north of Athens. Penn reduced his speed and hugged the right of the road.

Suddenly, a car roared up alongside them. Two men with shotguns leaned out the windows and fired. The first blast whizzed past Penn and out the opposite side of his car. But the second was right on target—making mincemeat of the Negro educator's face and head, splattering his blood and brains all over the car's roof and windshield.

Brown, awakened by the shooting, grabbed the wheel in time to keep the car under control. But, by the time he and Howard were able to realize fully what had happened, the murderers' car was out of sight.

News of the slaying reached Washington later that morning and the Federal Bureau of Investigation went into action immediately. Assistant F.B.I. Director J. J. Casper was dispatched personally to Georgia to head a team of sleuths who would "leave no stone unturned" in their search for the killers. State law enforcement agencies joined the probe, and Governor Carl Sanders declared that he would "not rest easy" until the murderers had been brought to justice.

At first, investigators found the going tough. If the people of Madison and Clarke Counties knew anything about the murder, they were unwilling to talk. Gradually, however, clues began falling neatly into place —pointing to four Athens men, all members of the Ku Klux Klan.

The men were:

Joseph Howard Sims, 41-year-old father of six, a machinist and a Navy combat veteran. Several months before, he had been arrested for pointing a pistol at civil rights demonstrators.

Hubert Guest, 37-year-old garage operator and gun collector. Married but childless, Guest had previously been arrested on June 21, 1964, after shots had been fired into a Negro's home, wounding two persons. He had been found guilty of disorderly conduct and fined $105.

Cecil William Myers, 25-year-old father of three, a yarn plucker by trade. He, like Sims and Guest, was a long-time Athens resident and had been an outspoken foe of the Negro civil rights movement.

James Lackey, 29-year-old service station attendant. Married but childless, and a newcomer to Athens. Since his arrival, he had been "thick" with the other three Klansmen.

According to F.B.I. Director J. Edgar Hoover, the garage of gun-collector Guest was a "frequent gathering place for Myers, Sims, Lackey and other members" of the Klan. When F.B.I. agents visited the garage, they found a number of weapons hanging on the wall— including a sawed-off shotgun and a high-powered rifle.

Thomas E. Folendore, an 18-year-old member of the Klan, told investigators that he saw Sims, Myers and Lackey carrying shotguns into Guest's garage at approximately 5 a.m. on the morning of the shooting. He also stated that several days after the shooting, Sims had asked him if the F.B.I. had questioned him.

"Watch what you say [to them]," the youth quoted Sims as having warned him.

On August 16, 1964—less than a month after Penn had met his bloody death—Federal agents arrested all four men on charges of violating the Civil Rights Act of 1964 as well as a civil rights law enacted during the Reconstruction era. Two of the men were already at the F.B.I. temporary headquarters in the Athens Post Office when the arrest warrants were issued; a third was picked up at his home; and the fourth, Sims, was arrested at Clarke County Klavern, the K.K.K.'s Athens headquarters.

All four were charged in the F.B.I.'s formal complaint with having conspired "with each other, and with others unknown, to injure, oppress, threaten and intimidate members of the Negro race," specifically Penn and his two companions, for the purpose of preventing "such citizens from exercising the rights secured to them."

Moreover, the complaint continued, Sims, Myers and Lackey "did shoot and kill Lemuel Penn"—and Guest permitted his garage to be used as a "frequent gathering place" by these three and by "other members of the United Klans of America, Inc., Knights of the Ku Klux Klan."

The charges, it was pointed out, were addressed to the civil rights statutes—which carry a maximum penalty of 10 years' imprisonment—because murder violates no Federal law. Two days later, the state of Georgia filed murder charges. Now, if indicted by a Madison County grand jury, the four could be tried for murder in the first degree—and, if convicted, could face the death penalty.

Said Governor Sanders when the arrests were announced:

"I want to congratulate the Georgia Bureau of Investigation, the Federal Bureau of Investigation and all the other law officers who have participated in this investigation.

"If those arrested are determined to be responsible for the crime, they will be dealt with properly in the courts.

"Further, if they are responsible, I want to extend my sympathy to their families—the same as I did to

that of the murdered man—because it will be those
families who will have to bear the burden of this non-
sensible act."

On August 25, 1964, the grand jury convened to
weigh state's evidence and determine if the four should
be brought to trial before a jury of their peers. Testimony was offered by F.B.I. agents, by Sheriff Dewey
Seagraves and by Penn's passengers, Brown and Howard. Based on this testimony, indictments were returned
against Sims, Myers and Lackey.

Now, it was up to the state of Georgia to convince
a panel of 12 citizens that the three were guilty as
charged. Solicitor-General Clete Johnson took personal
charge of the prosecution and made it clear that he
would demand the death penalty.

Little did anyone realize it at the time, but Johnson
had at his disposal as damning a bit of evidence as has
ever been presented in a courtroom—the signed confession of one of the three men!

> "At some time between 4 a.m. and 4:30 a.m.,
> we spotted a 1959 Chevy occupied by several col-
> ored men. We trailed the car and noticed the
> Washington, D. C., plates. I believe Mr. Sims said:
> " 'THAT MUST BE SOME OF PRESIDENT
> JOHNSON'S BOYS.'
>
> "I was driving, and I began following the car as
> directed by Myers, who was sitting alongside of me
> up front. Sims was sitting in the back.
>
> "Sims told me to fall back and follow the Ne-
> groes, and I stayed back 100 to 200 yards. I asked
> the others what they were going to do, and Sims
> said:
> " 'I'M GOING TO KILL ME A NIGGER.'
>
> "Both Sims and Myers told me to pass the car
> occupied by the Negroes from Washington. When I
> came alongside the Negroes' car, both Myers and
> Sims fired shotguns into the Negroes' car.
>
> "The double-barrel shotgun used by Cecil Myers
> was the shotgun usually hanging on the wall of

Guest's garage. The shotgun used by Sims is his own.

"As soon as we got back to Guest's garage, both Myers and Sims cleaned the shotguns in the garage. They wiped the guns off with a rag.

"Guest asked what had happened, and Sims said:

"'WE SHOT ONE, BUT DON'T KNOW IF WE KILLED HIM OR NOT.'"

Under questioning by the F. B. I. agents, Lackey had spelled out the trio's "reasons" for shooting Penn. His testimony in this regard had been incorporated into the confession. It reads:

"The original reason for our following the colored men was because we heard that Martin Luther King might make Georgia a testing ground for the civil rights bill.

"We thought some out-of-town niggers might stir up some trouble in Athens. We had intended scaring off any out-of-town colored people before they could give us any trouble.

"When the car from Washington was spotted on July 11, we thought they might be out-of-towners who might cause trouble."

Also at the disposal of Solicitor-General Johnson was the statement given F.B.I. agents by garage-owner Guest.

"They (Sims and Myers) told me they were the ones that shot at the car in which Penn was killed," he said.

After turning state's evidence, Lackey was granted a separate trial. Sims and Myers were then scheduled to go before a jury at Danielsville as co-defendants in a first degree murder trial.

Solicitor-General Johnson, armed with the Lackey confession and the Guest statement—to say nothing of the testimony of F.B.I. agents, local law enforcement officers and "civilian" witnesses—seemed to have an airtight case. But, if he did not appear terribly optimistic as he took his seat behind the prosecution table on the first day of the trial, it soon would be apparent why . . .

Madison County Courthouse in Danielsville, Ga., is a sprawling, weather-beaten structure with large windows and an immense Romanesque door. Its first floor is given over entirely to administrative offices. Its second is dominated by a huge, double-decker, racially segregated courtroom.

It was hot and humid in this second-story courtroom on September 2, 1964—so hot and humid that the thick, dirt-gray walls appeared to perspire. And yet, the place was packed. A capacity crowd of newsmen, local people and visiting curiosity-seekers grappled for seats in the "Whites Only" section facing the judge's bench. Directly above, a sardine-thick regiment of sad-faced Negroes stood vigil in the narrow balcony set aside for "Coloreds." They all had come to see the trial by jury of a pair of Ku Klux Klan members, accused of the vicious and unprovoked shotgun murder of a distinguished Negro educator who had been driving through their state.

At the prosecutor's table, Solicitor-General Clete Johnson huddled with Special State Prosecutor Jeff Wayne, a tall, wiry criminal lawyer from Gainsville, widely respected throughout the South for his skill in cross-examining uncooperative witnesses. Across the room, at the defense table, court appointed attorney James Hudson sat conferring with his 60-year-old colleague, John Darsey, known throughout the region as a fiery orator of the old school and an outspoken "States' rights" man.

With the bailiff's call of *"All rise!"* Judge William Carey Skelton entered the room and the trial of *State of Georgia v. Joseph Howard Sims and Cecil William Myers* was underway.

For two days, the opposing legal teams assaulted the jury with a barrage of contradictory evidence, testimony and argument. Principal source of contention was a confession extracted by the F.B.I. from accused conspirator John S. Lackey. Defense attorney Hudson contended the eight page, hand-written document should not be admitted as evidence; Special Prosecutor Wayne maintained it should. After listening to the arguments, Judge Skelton ruled in favor of the prosecution.

"I'll admit it," he said.

Wayne then read the confession aloud. An audible gasp rose from the Negroes' balcony when he came to the part where Lackey quoted Sims as saying:

"I'm going to kill me a nigger."

Now, defense attorney Hudson introduced an opposing statement—in which the accused conspirator repudiated the confession and said that he had been harassed by the F.B.I. into making it. The defendants grinned broadly in their seats.

The prosecution then introduced the statement of Hubert Guest that Sims and Myers had told him they killed Penn. Also introduced was Guest's account of a conversation he overheard between Sims and Myers: "I overhead one of them say that they thought the car they had shot had gone into the river."

Guest took the stand himself to repudiate these statements. He told the jury that he was sick, hungry and faint during the F.B.I. questioning and that he could not remember signing any statement. Under Wayne's cross-examination, he took the Fifth Amendment a total of 16 times.

The prosecution produced Thomas Folendore, who testified that he had seen Sims and Myers carrying sawed-off shotguns with pistol handles into Guest's garage on the morning of the crime. The testimony was corroborated by Claude Bennet, an employee at the garage, who said that he also had seen the duo enter the building with the weapons in their hands.

To contradict this testimony, the defense produced a group of witnesses who swore that they had seen Sims and Myers in Athens on the morning of the crime. The key witness in the group was Landys Moore, a Negro girl who worked at an all-night diner. She said she had seen Sims and Myers together not once, but twice—shortly after midnight and again about 5 a.m.

Prosecutor Wayne pointed out that this did not necessarily mean that the two could not have committed the crime—nor did it invalidate the testimony of the state witnesses. Athens was only 10 miles from the scene of the crime, he reminded the jury; Sims and Myers could have made their appearances at the diner and still have shot Penn and cleaned their weapons at Guest's garage.

In a particularly dramatic moment during the cross-examination of Landys Moore, Wayne demanded that the Negro girl tell the jury what Sims and Myers were wearing when she saw them.

"They were wearing guns and holsters," she admitted.

On the third day, the state rested its case. Hudson and Darsey then made a one-hour-and-forty-minute presentation in which Sims and Myers declared their innocence.

"I believe I was in Athens at this time," a sober-faced Sims told the jury.

Echoed Myers:

"I do believe I was in Athens at this time."

Now, it was time for the closing arguments. Special Prosecutor Wayne warned the jurors that if Sims and Myers were acquitted in the face of overwhelming evidence, it would mean that the killing was being condoned and that "human life has less value than a box of snuff."

Solicitor-General Johnson declared that Penn was slain with a "motive of hate and violence" and demanded the death penalty.

"This is an extreme case and demands the extreme penalty," he charged. "It was cold-blooded assassination . . . Lemuel Penn was born a Negro. He came into this world with a black skin. Is that a crime? Something ought to be done to stop this night-riding with pistols and shotguns."

Speaking for the defense, Attorney Darsey offered what the Associated Press termed "a rafter-ringing, arm-waving argument that left him on the verge of exhaustion."

Ignoring completely the evidence in the case, he accused the Federal Government of "carpet-bagging administration of justice" and hammered away at the racial issue and states' rights theme.

"They loosed a horde of Federal agents in our midst," he charged, pounding the jury box with his fist. "President Johnson sent them swarming in" with an order not to "come back until you bring us white meat."

Darsey assailed the civil rights movement for "plaguing" the nation with "sit-ins, sit-downs, walk-ins, walk-outs . . . insurrections, riots, police dogs, fire hoses, U. S. marshals and Federal troops."

Then he lashed out bitterly at the Johnson Administration for passing the Civil Rights Act of 1964.

"They may succeed in passing forced laws," he said. "They may get them upheld and ruled constitutional by the Supreme Court. They may break down the distinction between Federal jurisdiction and states' rights. But in the name of all that's holy . . . they shall never destroy the jury system, which is the heart and soul of Anglo-Saxon jurisprudence."

Pacing back and forth in front of the jury box, he suggested that Sims and Myers were victims of a Federal attempt to appease militant Negroes.

"Never let it be said," he boomed, "that a Madison County jury converted an electric chair into a sacrificial altar on which the pure flesh of a member of the human race was sacrificed to the savage, revengeful appetite of a raging mob."

His shoulders sagging and his thin, white hair disheveled, the volatile Darsey made his way back to the defense table. Small smiles of satisfaction showed on the faces of his clients. A ripple of appreciative murmurs spread throughout the crowd in the "Whites Only" section.

Judge Skelton briefly instructed the jurors on the legal aspects of the case. The 12-member panel—all male and all Caucasian—then retired for deliberations. Up in the narrow balcony set aside for "coloreds," there was no suspense as to the outcome of these deliberations. Slowly and silently, the Negroes—who had been observing the proceedings since the opening day—filed out of the courtroom, one by one, looking very much like pallbearers who had come to mourn at the wrong funeral.

*　　*　　*

The Georgia sun had set, and a cool, evening breeze was blowing through the open windows of the courtroom. From the street outside came the sounds of traffic, of children playing, and of a teen-ager's transistor radio.

The 12 jurors, having deliberated for three hours and fifteen minutes, were led back into the jury box. Judge Skelton rapped the bench with his gavel and a hush fell over the room.

"Have you reached a verdict?" the judge asked.

The foreman of the jury stood and cleared his throat.

"We have, Your Honor."

"How do you find the defendants?"

"Not guilty."

The audience in the "Whites Only" section broke into cheers and applause. Some men, beaming happily, clapped each other on the back with enthusiasm. The judge pounded his gavel to restore order.

At the defense table, Sims and Myers—along with their attorneys, Hudson and Darsey—were jubilant. Hudson later told reporters, in effect, he considered the verdict a clear-cut defeat of the Federal Government. "We stand ready to fight the Federal Government again!" he declared, referring to the Civil Rights Act violation his clients were still charged with.

Asked how his clients might meet the $25,000 bonds set against them by U. S. Commissioner Girard Hawkins, he flashed a smile and replied:

"These boys got a lot of friends and we do, too."

Solicitor-General Johnson made no attempt to conceal his dissatisfaction with the outcome of the case. "I'm disappointed," he said. "We left no stones unturned, but the jury had the last say."

As news of the acquittal spread throughout Danielsville and Athens, men (and women) congratulated each other and leaped excitedly up and down the streets. After their arrest by the F.B.I. on August 6, Sims, Myers, Lackey and Guest had been promptly expelled from the Ku Klux Klan. Now, the jury's verdict was regarded by some, not only as an acquittal of the accused murderers, but also as an endorsement in a court of law of the Klan itself. Remarked one Georgian, who proudly identified himself as a Klansman:

"After 100 years, we've finally had our day in court. It was a long time coming."

Sims and Myers, outside the courtroom where they had just been found innocent, posed with their wives for photographers.

"I'm overjoyed!" declared an exuberant Mrs. Sims. "I've prayed for this."

Her husband, meanwhile, took advantage of the occasion to get in a plug for the Klan from which he had just been expelled—but to whose beliefs he evidently still subscribed.

"The Klan," he declared, "is the most *dedicated* organization in America. It's fifty percent more religious than the churches in Athens. You have to be white, gentile and born in America to be a member of the Klan. You have to be a *real* American."

And, a few days later, National Ku Klux Klan Imperial Wizard James Venable gloated to reporters at Atlanta:

"You'll never be able to convict a white man that kills a nigger what encroaches on the white race of the South."

12

OPERATION: INFILTRATION

"The only agency that sought the bodies or the murderers was the F.B.I. State highway patrolmen gave verbal support. They stood on the riverbank and shouted advice to Bureau men who were working the boats:

"'If you want to find that damn nigger, just float a relief check out there. That black bastard will reach up and grab it!'"

WILLIAM BRADFORD HUIE,
Philadelphia, Miss., 1964

SHORTLY AFTER DAWN on the hot, muggy morning of June 21, 1964, three civil rights workers from the Council of Federal Organizations left their Meridian, Miss., headquarters to investigate the burning of a Negro church near Philadelphia, in Neshoba County.

Before departing, they were warned of the perils of the trip. Neshoba County was the heart of "seg" country. Racist sentiments ran high. As COFO rights workers, they would be special targets—particularly hated because two of them happened to be Caucasian "agitators" from "up North." Under no circumstances, they were told, should they remain in the area after sundown.

The trio—21-year-old James Chaney, a Negro from Meridian; 24-year-old Michael Schwerner and 20-year-old Andrew Goodman, Caucasians from New York—arrived at the church well ahead of schedule. They completed their visit before noon, jumped back into their blue station wagon and began the return trip to Meridian.

They never got there. Sometime during the afternoon, they were arrested on the outskirts of Philadelphia by Neshoba County Deputy Sheriff Cecil Price. He locked them up in the county jail on speeding charges and didn't release them until after dark. Then they disappeared. Two days later, their burned-out station wagon turned up in a Neshoba swamp.

COFO officials, fearing for the worst, pleaded for a Federal investigation. President Johnson, realizing that their fears were well founded, immediately put through a call to J. Edgar Hoover. Within hours, a 153-man undercover army was placed in operation. Named as its commander was 50-year-old Roy K. Moore, a 26-year F.B.I. veteran. The order went out: Find the bodies!

The logical place for the investigation to begin was with the last known man to see the rights workers alive, Deputy Sheriff Price. Moore had him picked up for questioning.

Price, a fat-faced, rat-eyed redneck with a 46-inch waist and an I.Q. to match, played it even dumber than he looked. He had jailed the three youths, he said, until he got word from Sheriff Lawrence Rainey to release them. Then he escorted them to the edge of town, where he watched them drive out of sight.

The story was full of holes and the G-men knew it. Price might be a dunce, but he couldn't be *that* stupid. Since when did deputy sheriffs start locking up traffic violators on an open charge? Was it customary to deny speeders the right to make a phone call? Why weren't the youths permitted to post bond? *And since when does an arresting officer hold not only the driver of a car on traffic charges but his passengers as well?*

Price couldn't answer the questions, but he wouldn't confess to any hanky-panky. He might have made a mistake in arresting the kids, he conceded. But that's all it was—a mistake. He *thought* he was doing the right thing.

Sheriff Rainey was no more helpful. Stuffing his enormous mouth with an oversized chaw of Red Man tobacco, he answered F.B.I. questions with meaningless gulps and pig-like grunts. He was "out of town" when the action took place, he averred; therefore he couldn't be held responsible. Besides, the "nigger" an' the two "nigger-lovers" prob'ly warn't daid, anyhow. Yuh cain't say 'ere's been a murder lessen y'all got one of 'em 'ere *corpus delecti's,* now, can yuh?

Faced with similar open hostility on all sides, F.B.I. Task Force Commander Moore intensified efforts in the technical areas. Previously, Bureau Headquarters at Jackson had been a floor and a half of empty office space; now it became a bustling command post, complete with clattering teletypes, gun and ammunition lockers, interview rooms, extensive laboratory facilities and a 10,000-entry mug-and-fingerprint file. Aerial photographs of Neshoba County were scanned for possible changes in landscape which might indicate the victims' graves. Meanwhile, helicopters conducted a personal, tree-top reconnaissance and a mixed force of G-men and U. S. Navy personnel probed the Neshoba swamplands in boats and on foot.

The official attitude to all this activity was one of injured innocence. The mayor of Philadelphia refused to believe that a crime had been committed. United Klans' Imperial Wizard Robert N. Shelton, arriving from Tuscaloosa for an "inspection tour," charged that the whole affair was a fraud; he promised: *"my* people will continue the investigation." And at Jackson, Governor Paul Johnson expressed grave doubts that the three young men were not still alive. As William Bradford Huie characterized the Mississippi attitude for *The New York Herald Tribune*: "It was all a hoax . . . And, if there had been a crime, it wasn't really a crime because the victims were the guilty parties: They had 'asked for it.' "

From on the scene in Philadelphia, Huie also provided this chilling report: "The only agency that sought the bodies or the murderers was the F.B.I. State highway patrolmen gave verbal support. They stood on the riverbank and shouted advice to the F.B.I. men who were working the boats:

"If you want to find that damn nigger, just float a relief check out there. That black bastard will reach up and grab it!"

* * *

As reports reached Washington that the F.B.I. was single-handedly fighting the organized resistance of an entire state, J. Edgar Hoover made a decision: the Kluxers must be got at from within; the Bureau would have to *infiltrate* the Klan precisely as it had infiltrated the Communist party!

Word was passed down through channels. OPERATION: INFILTRATION was begun. Before long, scenes like these were being enacted all over Mississippi:

* * *

A cool breeze blows over the swamp as the two men paddle the canoe toward shore. They are on a weekend camping trip and they are great friends— so ONE of them thinks.

The man in the front of the canoe is an F.B.I. man. He is also a local insurance agent. His companion knows only about the insurance agent part. That's why he's been trying to recruit him for the local K.K.K. Klavern.

The G-man does not appear too interested in the Klan. Only after many weeks does he permit himself to be "persuaded" to join. His new-found Klansmen "friends" think they have a genuine convert. They don't ever learn the truth—not even after his sleuthing puts them behind bars . . .

* * *

The singer groans noisily to life and the twangy guitars reverberate through the massive bass speakers. Next to the jukebox, an ex-Marine from Chicago sits nursing a beer. It is 3 a.m. and the bartender is yawning. But the ex-Marine is wide awake. He has to be. F.B.I. men don't sleep on the job.

At 3:15, an officer from the state's largest Klan unit pushes open the door and swaggers toward the jukebox. He hands the F.B.I. man an envelope containing top secret information about the K.K.K. In return the F.B.I. man hands him an envelope containing money.

The Klansman, who has just sold some of his best buddies down the river, now swaggers back out of the bar. Men don't swagger unless they're scared. This Klansman has good reason to be scared. He is one of only five men who had access to the information he just sold. He has, in effect, just bet his life that, when the sale is discovered, one of the other four will be thought the traitor.

There are other causes for concern, too. Maybe the G-men, after getting what they want from him, will throw him to the wolves. Maybe the money he just received is marked with special chemicals and his hands will turn purple an hour after he touches it. Maybe the yawning bartender, who is a cousin of the local police chief, will suspect what went on—and the Klansman will get shot in his own bed.

The F.B.I. man, meanwhile, walks out of the bar and returns to his headquarters. Once again he has received proof of the fallacy of an old chiché. There's honor among thieves? Like hell there is!

*   *   *

The ancient red pickup truck pulls to the side of the narrow dirt road and comes to a halt. There is silence for a moment. Then, from the woods nearby, a man whistles. The truck blinks its lights in reply.

The man in the woods silently lifts a package

from the ground and tucks it under his arm. Then he picks his way through the dense brush to the road. The door to the truck swings open as he approaches. He climbs inside.

The driver of the truck wears a heavy black overcoat. It is chilly outside, but not that chilly. The overcoat is for concealment, not warmth. Beneath it is a long white robe with a red circle over the heart; superimposed on the circle is a white cross; superimposed on the cross is a red diamond, inside of which is a small, flame-like symbol.

As the pickup truck moves toward a main highway, the passenger unwraps his package. It contains a white robe like that of his friend. He waits until the truck has stopped in a woodland clearing, then puts the robe on.

Now the two men walk down a path to a shack. Inside are a dozen other robed Klansmen. One of them wears a green robe with fancy embroidery. He is the Grand Dragon.

Neither the Grand Dragon nor his subordinates realize that one of the two men who have just entered is a spy. Even the other man—the man who accompanied the spy—is unaware of it.

The meeting begins and the Klansmen listen to the Grand Dragon's speech. The spy listens most closely of all . . .

Thus continued OPERATION: INFILTRATION— and, forty-four days after the investigation of the triple murders began, the F.B.I. found the bodies. No one believed it could be done—least of all the local "law enforcement" officers who actually *impeded* the search. But it was done—and, in such a manner as to make it clear that it wasn't just a lucky accident.

The bodies had been buried in the center of a 250-acre farm. They lay in hardened red clay 14 feet and 10 inches below the surface of a newly constructed dam. The Bureau could have used bulldozers and steam shovels, and torn apart the farm in stages, ultimately "stumbling" upon the bodies. This would have concealed the fact that there had been a tipoff by an informer—an informer very close to the murderers.

But the G-men *wanted* it known that they had been tipped off. So they erected a dragline in the middle of the dam and dug a precise letter V, at the nadir of which was the triple grave. The operation couldn't have been more precise.

Now, official notice had been served on the Kluxers. Their highly touted secrecy was a myth. Klansmen *could* be bought. Klansmen *had been* bought. Klansmen *would be* bought again!

*   *   *

On December 4, 1964, tobacco-chewing Sheriff Lawrence Rainey and his blimp-shaped deputy Cecil Price pulled their squad car to a halt in front of the Philadelphia courthouse. They had just returned from a predawn moonshine raid out in the boondocks and their trouser legs were still wet from the dewy grass. Their plan was to change clothes, then make a routine inspection of the jail cells. As things happened, the plan never came off.

No sooner had the 41-year-old Rainey and the 26-year-old Price entered their office than a quartet of trenchcoat-clad F.B.I. men marched in and placed them under arrest. Simultaneously, a 60-man army of Bureau agents fanned out through Neshoba and made 19 more arrests. By noon, all twenty-one were locked up at the Meridian Naval Air Station. Nineteen were charged with violating the Civil Rights Act of 1870, the other two with knowing about the crime and failing to report it. J. Edgar Hoover made official note that most of the arrested men were members or sympathizers of the Klan; one, 46-year-old Frank J. Herndon, was identified as Exalted Cyclops of the Meridian Klavern.

According to the charge sheet, *"it was part of the plan and purpose of the conspiracy that Cecil Ray Price, acting under the color of his office,"* would arrest the three COFO rights workers *"without lawful cause"* and *"de-*

tain them in the Neshoba County jail." Later, the charge continued, Price delivered the youths to his Klan buddies, who forced them into cars, drove them to a woodland on the edge of the town, beat them to near-death, finished the job with guns, hauled the bodies to Old Jolly Farm in Philadelphia and buried them in a shallow grave.

Charged with actually taking part in the murders were Deputy Price; Travis M. Barnette, 36, a garage operator; Horace Barnette, 25, a salesman; Jimmy Arledge, 27, a truck driver; Alton Wayne Roberts, 26, a salesman; Jimmy Snowden, 31, a truck driver; James E. Jordan, 38, a construction worker; Billy Wayne Posey, 28, a gas station attendant: Jerry Sharpe, 21, a lumber company manager, and Jimmy Lee Townsend, 17, a gas station attendant.

Charged as being connected with the conspiracy—and thus, under law, equally guilty—were Sheriff Rainey; Exalted Cyclops Herndon; Philadelphia policeman Otha Neal Burkes; and the Rev. Edgar Killen, a Free Will Baptist minister. Killen was described as a "fire and brimstone preacher" of the Connie Lynch school.

Brought before U. S. Commissioner Esther Carter, a Mississippi-born spinster unencumbered by even a modicum of legal training, the 19 alleged conspirators were ordered held in $5,000 bond; the other two suspects were held in $3,500 bond. All of them posted it promptly. Sheriff Rainey and Deputy Price were back at work in the courthouse by 5 o'clock that afternoon.

A week later, the 19 alleged conspirators were brought before Commissioner Carter for a preliminary hearing—a formality in which, once the prosecution establishes a *prima facie* case, previous charges are normally continued while a Federal grand jury decides whether or not indictments should be brought.

U. S. Justice Department Attorney Robert Owen lead with trump—the testimony of an F.B.I. Special Agent that one of the accused, Horace Barnette, had signed a confession. But Owen had barely finished his sentence when the 14 defense attorneys leaped up—virtually in unison—and objected that "hearsay" evidence was inadmissible. Commissioner Carter then, as if on cue, announced: "I will have to sustain the objection of the defendant. I don't think it would be admissible."

Owen was almost speechless. The commissioner's ruling was without precedent in the history of American jurisprudence. "The issue is not whether there should be an *indictment*," the U. S. attorney argued. "The issue before the commissioner is whether or not there is a *probability* that a crime has been committed and that these people committed it!"

But Miss Carter—like an actress who had memorized the script—wouldn't budge. The testimony was deemed inadmissible and the charges were dismissed.

In January of 1965, U. S. Assistant Attorney General John Doar bypassed the U. S. Commissioner's office and took the case directly to the Mississippi grand jury. Offered in evidence were confessions from two of the men who had been in the crowd which watched while the three civil rights workers were beaten and bludgeoned to death.

The grand jury promptly indicted Sheriff Rainey, Deputy Price and 16 others on charges of "Conspiracy Against Rights of Citizens." (The pertinent 1870 law reads: "If two or more persons conspire to injure, oppress, threaten or intimidate any citizen in the free exercise or enjoyment of any right or privilege secured to him by the Constitution or Laws of the United States . . . they shall be fined not more than $5,000 or imprisoned not more than ten years, or both.") All were freed on bond pending trial.

The indictments, of course, hardly represented a triumph for the Justice Department. The alleged conspirators still had to be tried by a jury of their *peers*— and Mississippi juries are not famous for convicting Caucasians accused of impinging upon the rights of Negroes . . . or "nigger-lovers."

Furthermore, the *State* of Mississippi—which could have brought murder charges, punishable by death, against all 18—simply refused to do so. Thus, for all intents and purposes, *if* the alleged conspirators actually *were* responsible for the deaths of Chaney, Schwerner and Goodman, they got away literally with murder.

Yet, the triple slaying of the rights workers was not a total victory for the Ku Klux Klan. The very fact that the F.B.I. was able, in the face of a statewide conspiracy of silence, to make 21 *arrests* is proof enough of the success of OPERATION: INFILTRATION. And the increased success of the operation would be evidenced again and again in the future.

On February 8, 1965, a K.K.K. knockoff squad met in Georgia to plot the murder of Martin Luther King. On February 9, the F.B.I. knew about it. Justice Department agents saw to it that King did not become a target for execution either on February 15, in Marion, Ala., or on February 26, in Hollywood, Calif.——the knockoff squad's two D-Days.

The only appeasement the Kluxers had was the bland (and seemingly blind) denial of Imperial Wizard Robert N. Shelton: "We don't want . . . leaders to satisfy that excited emotional feeling that can stomp and talk at meetings and then they'll go out and beat up or kill a nigger. No—we wish to provide satisfaction in a more constructive manner . . . I firmly believe that M. L. King will be eliminated by his own people—will be assassinated."

Another knockoff squad attempt failed when an F.B.I. shortwave radio message cut short the plans of Georgia Klansmen's crew, "The Secret Six," to assassinate Morris Abrams, president of the American Jewish Committee, "who would get his in New York"; vice-mayor Sam Massel, of Atlanta; and a Southern white clergyman.

All told, F.B.I. infiltrators have learned, there are 13 Klans operating in 11 states. The largest is Shelton's United Klans with 5,000 hard-core members. Next comes Mississippi's White Knights of the Ku Klux Klan with 2,000; then Louisiana's Original Knights of the Ku Klux Klan with 1,000, and United Florida Klans, with 1,000. The Association of South Carolina Klans is good for 500, while the remaining eight Klans share the remaining 500 Klansmen.

Significantly, the four men arrested for the murder of Lemuel Penn and those seized for the murder of Viola Liuzzo are all members of Shelton's United Klans. The alleged killers in each case comprised what Kluxers call "Violent Action Groups," officially, and "knockoff squads" unofficially. The individual squads—sort of a Gestapo within a Klan—operate outside the regular K.K.K. organizations, meet separately and are used as an inner police force to keep the rank and file in line. Some of the individual squads are the "Holy Terrors," the "Enforcers," the "K.B.I." (Klan Bureau of Investigation), and the "Security Patrol."

The extent to which the F.B.I. has these groups infiltrated was revealed when, after the Liuzzo slaying, Imperial Wizard Shelton himself complained that G-men had won over one Kluxer by offering him $160,000 to "sign a statement" and promising to move the man and his family "to a 500-acre farm in Minnesota to get him safely out of the South if he cooperated."

Were the circumstances surrounding the utterance not so tragic, it would have been ludicrous. Here was the Imperial Wizard of the Ku Klux Klan protesting officially that the U. S. Federal Bureau of Investigation had corrupted one of the members of a Klan knockoff squad! This is like killing your mother and father, then begging mercy on the grounds that you're an orphan. . . .

Yes, OPERATION: INFILTRATION was indeed a success!

13

K.K.K. ON THE CARPET

"The weapons of the Klan are secrecy, rumor and fear. Plain fact and simple truth, amply imparted to the public, are adequate remedies."
REP. CHARLES LONGSTREET WELTNER,
Washington, D. C., 1965

THE FLOOR of the United States House of Representatives was only half full and the public galleries were nearly empty. Speaker John C. McCormack had just made the last of the day's committee appointments. Now those few Congressmen who had bothered to show up for the session settled down to a long afternoon of speeches.

"Under previous order of the House," intoned McCormack, "the gentleman from Georgia is recognized for thirty minutes."

As tall, lean and youthful-looking Charles Longstreet Weltner rose to speak, a ripple of anticipation crossed the floor. Generally fellow Congressmen—especially the 20- and 25-year men—had little interest in the speech of a "second termer." But Weltner was no ordinary second termer. Not quite a year earlier, when the Civil Rights Act of 1964 had come up for a final vote, he startled the Congress—and the country—by being the only legislator from the "deep South"—

Senator or Representative—to vote for it. And today, his topic was: "The 100th Anniversary of the Ku Klux Klan."

"Mr. Speaker," he began in a crisp, clear voice with just a touch of a back-home accent, "the year 1965 marks the 100th anniversary of the Ku Klux Klan. In December a century ago, six young men formed a secret society in Pulaski, Tenn. The weird panoply of the order—along with the rigors of that day—quickly changed the Klan into a vehicle of terror. Soon excesses compelled its leaders to order it dismembered.

"That was in 1869. For almost five decades thereafter, the Ku Klux Klan was but a memory. Then, in 1915, a new order arose in Atlanta, based upon old hatreds and fears.

"The revised Klan found fertile ground, not only in the old Confederacy, but North, East and West alike. In 1921, the House Committee on Rules considered several resolutions calling for an investigation. Nothing happened. By 1924, membership in this 'invisible empire' reached four million. Its influence touched courthouses and Statehouses, national conventions of both major parties and Congress itself. It grew and prospered on mystery and malice, changing the cross from the symbol of hope to a sign of hate.

"For over a quarter century following its rebirth, the Klan was a potent factor in American life. But the Second World War brought sharp decline to the 'invisible empire.' Once again it slumbered— until the Supreme Court's [school desegregation] decision of 1954. Since that date, but most significantly during the past two years, Klan manifestations have increased throughout the South. There are now visible signs of a westward spread."

Weltner cleared his throat. His colleagues watched intently. The peroration was over. Now it was time for the meat of the speech.

"Mr. Speaker," continued the 37-year-old Congressman, "all this comes at a critical time for the South. We are rising to our full potential. We are struggling for orderly progress. We are turning to real problems and solid opportunities.

"*Yet, once again, this madness is in our midst. It impugns a lawful and generous people. It impairs compliance with the law. It impedes administration of justice* . . .

"What shall be done?

"Shall we in the Congress ignore the veil of fear descending upon whole communities? Shall we permit faceless men, under cover of robes and darkness, to imperil the liberties of our people?

"I believe I speak for a vast majority of southerners in calling for action. For in doing nothing, we will inaugurate a second century for the Ku Klux Klan."

By this point, even some of the old-timers were sitting on the edge of their seats. Weltner had called for Congressional *action*. Did that mean an investigation? And, if so—by whom?

"The House Committee on Unamerican Activities," thundered Weltner, "is charged to investigate 'the extent, character and objects of Unamerican propaganda activities in the United States.' Honest men may differ on the precise limitations of the word Unamerican. But, surely, all will agree that activities which by force and violence seek to deprive others of rights guaranteed them by the Constitution *are Un-A-merican!*

"The weapons of the Klan are secrecy, rumor and fear. Plain fact and simple truth, amply imparted to the public, are adequate remedies. This committee can provide these remedies by thorough and detailed investigation."

A hush fell over the House. In less than five minutes, Weltner had broken 100 years of precedent. Not only had he, as a Caucasian Southerner, derided the Ku Klux Klan, but he had also demanded an investigation of the hooded order by what was traditionally one of the most radically conservative committees in Congress— the House Unamerican Activities Committee!

Now Weltner had the undivided attention of the entire floor. Even the traditionally noisy galleries were death-still.

"Let us turn upon this 'invisible empire' the light of public scrutiny," he demanded. "Let us examine in full its extent, character and objects. Let us reveal for all to see the men behind the masks.

"The boast of the Klan—'Yesterday, Today and Tomorrow'—is true in part. For the Klan of yesterday is the Klan of today. Its means and methods remain unchanged. It will plague us tomorrow unless we quash it today.

"The year 1865 witnessed the birth of the Ku Klux Klan. Let the year 1965 witness its final demise."

No sooner had he finished the sentence than Representative George W. Grider was on his feet requesting recognition.

"Mr. Speaker," he declared, "I think it is fitting and appropriate that another southern member of this body rise to endorse the excellent words of the gentleman from Georgia . . . I believe that this is a proper subject for the House Committee on Unamerican Activities to investigate, and I heartily endorse the suggestion of my colleague . . ."

* * *

Though warmly received on the House floor, Weltner's call for an HUAC investigation of the Klan soon seemed destined to die a quiet death. The matter was taken "under advisement," then was all but forgotten.

Ironically, it *might* have been forgotten completely had Kluxers kept their hooded noses clean. But, with the savage highway-murder of Mrs. Viola Liuzzo, the K.K.K. was thrust into the national spotlight as never before. And, when it was revealed that Gary Rowe, one of the four Klansmen originally arrested in connection with the slaying, was in fact an F.B.I. informant who had infiltrated an Alabama Konklave five years earlier and who had been spying on his sheeted brethren ever since, the result was near pandemonium.

In May of 1965, Rowe became the prosecution's star witness in the murder trial of Collie Leroy Wilkins. (The other two alleged conspirators, Eugene Thomas and

William Orville Eaton, were scheduled for trial later in the year.) Testifying that he had ridden around in the murder car all night and most of the day, the stocky F.B.I. informant told a packed courtroom in the Lowndes County courthouse of Hayneville, Ala. that he had seen Wilkins fire the fatal shots—and that he had heard him boast afterwards: "Baby Brother, I don't miss. That so-and-so is dead and in hell."

Rowe began his narrative about Mrs. Liuzzo's last hours in a low, emotionless voice. "We pulled up to a red light," he said, "and there was an auto to our left. Wilkins said, 'Look over there, Baby Brother.' He said, 'I'll be damned, look over there!' And we all looked and saw them together [Mrs. Liuzzo and Negro rightsworker Leroy Moton]. Gene Thomas said, 'Let's get them.' Mr. Eaton added, 'Wonder where they're going.' Gene Thomas stated, 'Well, I imagine they are going out there to park someplace together.' "

Following Mrs. Liuzzo's car onto Highway 80, Rowe continued, Klansman Thomas "reached over and got his revolver out from beneath the seats and said, 'Get your pistols, cousins.' " It was at this point, said Rowe, that he first tried to persuade Thomas to turn back. "Naw," Thomas allegedly replied, "we're going to take this car tonight."

As Mrs. Liuzzo picked up speed in a frantic attempt to outfox her pursuers, Rowe continued, the Klansmen's speedometer soared past 90; then Driver Thomas slowed down as he spotted two uniformed officers of the Alabama Highway Patrol ticketing a Volkswagen bus at the side of the road. When the policemen were out of sight, the chase resumed.

Again, Rowe stated, he tried to persuade Thomas not to go on. But Thomas replied irritably: "I done told you, Baby Brother, you're in the big time now. We're going to take that automobile." Then, said Rowe, he closed the gap.

Now a hush fell over the crowded courtroom as Rowe, in a chillingly soft but completely audible tone, described the finale:

"As we got almost even Wilkins said, 'Give it some

gas.' Gene sped up a little bit and put our auto immediately beside the driver. Wilkins put his arm out the window approximately elbow distance, and, just as we got even with the front window, there was the lady driving the automobile and she turned around and looked directly facing the automobile we were in. She looked directly at us. Just as she looked at us, Wilkins fired two shots through the window of the front of the automobile. Gene Thomas said, 'All right, men, shoot the hell out of it.' Everybody started shooting. I was on the side by Wilkins and Wilkins said, 'Here, put your gun out here,' and I laid my arm outside the window up beside Wilkins.' "

Rowe said that he followed Wilkins' instructions—but only pretended to fire his pistol. "Wilkins and Eaton," he added, "both emptied their revolvers toward the automobile." Then the foursome sped away.

A short distance down the road, Rowe said, "The automobile is following us now. I believe you missed." To which Wilkins allegedly replied: "Baby Brother, I don't miss. That so-and-so is dead and in hell."

But, astonishing though Rowe's testimony was, the highpoint of the trial undoubtedly was the venom-filled, 67-minute harangue by bulky defense attorney Matthew Hobson Murphy Jr., 51, a Kluxer himself and self-styled Imperial Klonsel of the United Klans of America. Pounding the defense table, shaking his fist in the air, strutting back and forth across the floor the red-faced Klonsel made so overt an appeal toward racial hatred that even avowed segregationists in the audience turned away in apparent disgust.

"And this white woman who got killed?!" he thundered, his white hair awry, his throat swollen in excitement. "White woman? Where's that N.A.A.C.P. card? I thought I'd never see the day when Communists and niggers and white niggers and Jews were flying under the banner of the United Nations flag, not the American flag we fought for . . . Do you know those big black niggers were driven by the woman, sitting in the back seat? Niggers! One white woman and these niggers.

Right there. Riding right through your county! Communists dominate them niggers . . ."

The hot-eyed Klonsel wheeled past the table on which sat the blood-spattered purse of Viola Liuzzo, found by police in her car shortly after the murder.

"I'm proud to be a white man and I'm proud to stand upon my feet for white supremacy," he screamed, glaring contemptuously at the blood-spattered purse—as if it, too, represented a threat to his wellbeing. "Not black supremacy, not the mixing and the mongrelization of races not . . . the Zionists that run that bunch of niggers. The white people are not going to run before them. And when white people join up to them, they become white niggers."

A vein in his temple throbbed wildly as he spun around and looked directly into the eyes of the jurors. "Integration breaks every moral law God ever wrote," he said. "Noah's son was Ham and he committed adultery and was banished and his sons were Hamites and God banished them and they went to Africa and the only thing they ever built was grass huts. No white woman can ever marry a descendent of Ham. That's God's law . . . I don't care what Lyndon Johnson or anybody else says . . ."

Returning briefly to the evidence which had been offered by the prosecution, Murphy sought to disqualify Rowe's testimony on the grounds that, if he was telling the truth, the F.B.I. informer was a party to the crime. Were his contention valid, it would be necessary for the prosecution to provide corroborating testimony from another witness. But he abandoned this rhetorical course in mid-sentence and returned quickly to the emotional imprecations with which he obviously felt so at home.

"What kind of a man is this Rowe that comes into a fraternal organization by hook or crook?" cried the Klonsel. "He cares not what he swears to, and let me say this, gentlemen: he took an oath when he joined the United Klans of America . . . He took this oath with his hand raised to Almighty God . . . Remember Judas Iscariot . . ."

Finally, he retreated once more to the old racist theme. "You know he's a liar and a perjurer, holding himself out to be a white man, and worse than a white nigger!"

The fires of Klokard oratory now stoked up within him, Murphy turned to the subject of Leroy Moton, who had testified for the prosecution that he was the Negro riding with Mrs. Liuzzo at the time she was slain.

"You know what that nigger said on the stand?" Murphy, with mock incredulity shouted to the jurors. "He said, 'No,' 'Yeah,' 'No,' 'Yeah.' Like a ten-year-old boy. He should have been saying 'Yes, sir,' and 'No, sir,' before that honorable white judge. But the buck hasn't got the sense, the morals or the decency . . . I said, 'Now look, boy. Look down at your feet.' Niggers only understand this kind of talk. 'How many feets away was that car?' So he looked down at his feet and said, 'About 25 feet away.' . . . He said, 'I passed out for 25 or 30 minutes.' What was he doing down there all that time? In that car—alone!—with that woman?!"

Shaking his fist in the air again, Murphy brought the diatribe to its vituperative conclusion. "The nigger ran up the road and a truck came by and he stopped it," he sneered. "There was a rabbi in that truck. A rabbi. Of course, he stopped and put the nigger in the back. And there they were—rabbi with a nigger . . . white woman . . . nigger man . . . nigger woman . . . all in there, feet to feet . . ."

Now limp with exhaustion, sweat-soaked Matthew Hobson Murphy Jr.—who hates to see his name in print as Matthew Hobson Murphy Jr.—lumbered back toward the defense table, and Alabama Assistant Attorney General Joseph B. Gantt, chief prosecutor, was left with the task of putting the issues back into perspective.

"I don't want to talk about the Communist Party, or the Teamsters Union, or the N.A.A.C.P. or segregation or integration or whites or niggers or marches or demonstrations," he said, alluding to a few of the many subjects which had found their way into Murphy's harangue. "I want to talk about a murder case that happened in Lowndes County."

Mrs. Viola Liuzzo was killed, he said, only because she was riding in the same car as a Negro just as many residents of the county ride with Negroes when they drive home their handymen, maids and cooks. "If that's grounds for murder, blood can flow in Lowndes County," he warned.

Taking issue with Murphy's claims of patriotism and courage, he stated that Klansman Wilkins had cold-bloodedly killed a defenseless woman. "Is that the kind of bravery we fought for?" he asked. "I'd say not."

Finally the case went to the jury—a twelve-man panel of mechanics, machinists, farmers, electricians and nightwatchmen headed by foreman Clifford Mc-Murphy. Eleven of the group were native Alabamans, the twelfth a Florida transplant.

For ten hours the jurors weighed the case, then reported a deadlock. Judge Thomas Werth Thagard sent them to Montgomery for a night's sleep, then urged them to try again. They tried—twice. But in the end foreman McMurphy was forced to announce an hopeless deadlock, ten-to-two for conviction on a charge of manslaughter. "We've been hung almost the same from the outset, judge," he said. "It's been right constant." Thagard declared a mistrial and Wilkins was slated to face once again later in the year the judgement of a jury of his peers.

To many observers the trial represented a most significant turning point. Indeed, one juror made it plain that he was outraged by Klonsel Murphy's racist diatribe.

"I think a great many of us were insulted to a great extent," said Edmund Salee, a farmer. "He must have thought we were very, very ignorant to be taken in by that act."

The sentiments were shared by columnist Murray Kempton, who in the *New York World-Telegram* noted sardonically: "If Collie Lee Wilkins had been convicted, he might be the first client in the history of law to have grounds for appeal on the plea of *dementia* of counsel."

Thus the trial of Collie Lee Wilkins. Whatever the final outcome, there can be little doubt that with the murder of Mrs. Viola Liuzzo the Klan has acquired more numerous and more formidable enemies than it had ever encountered in its 100-year history.

Declared the President of the United States at Washington, D.C.:

"I am asking and directing Attorney General Katzenbach to proceed at the earliest possible date to develop legislation that will bring the activities of the Klan under effective control of the law . . . And, in connection with new legislation, Congressional committees may wish to investigate the activities of such organizations and the part they play in instigating violence. And I hope that if the Congressional committees do decide to proceed forthwith, they can be assured of the cooperation of all patriotic Americans and certainly we will make all the resources of the Federal Government and the F.B.I. available to them."

In the House, salty veteran Representative Emmanual Celler from Brooklyn, Chairman of the Judiciary Committee, quickly promised that if HUAC wouldn't investigate the Klan, his committee most certainly would. "I'll give him an investigation with all possible dispatch," the fiery septuagenarian declared.

But HUAC Chairman Edwin E. Willis, of Louisiana, made it clear that that wouldn't be necessary. "Klanism is incompatible with Americanism," he declared flatly. And, with that, he promised "time, and effort, and a lot of hard digging."

The HUAC decision to investigate the Klan was both significant and symbolic. For not only were the author of the idea and the chairman of the committee southerners, but also five of its nine members. The Klan would be unmasked not by "carpet-bagger" Yankee liberals, but by responsible members of its own geographic community . . .

*   *   *

With the full force of the Federal Government now being brought against it, it may appear that the days of the Ku Klux Klan are numbered. But, as W. R. Pattangall observed more than a quarter century ago, the Ku Klux Klan is also a *state of mind*.

"You've got to understand," Imperial Wizard Robert N. Shelton in a moment of astonishing insight once told *The New York Post,* "a man just doesn't *join* the Klan. He's born with the Klan *in* him . . . It's a philosophy, a religion."

Yet, philosophies and religions often prove to be as transitory as humans. It may be impossible to *kill* an idea, but, as has been proved time and time again, from the Babylonian civilizations of 4,000 B. C. to the Christian civilizations of the post-Inquisition period, it *is* possible to *replace* an idea . . . with a better idea!

The flame of the torch of bigotry need not burn eternally. Its sickly glow will give way to the light of reason when the torch bearers can be made to see the truth—long ago held to be self-evident—that all men *are* created equal. Such a goal is not easily attainable. But neither is it unattainable. Merely by recognizing its desirability we have taken the all-important first step.